1 MONTH OF
FREE
READING

at

www.ForgottenBooks.com

By purchasing this book you are eligible for one month membership to ForgottenBooks.com, giving you unlimited access to our entire collection of over 700,000 titles via our web site and mobile apps.

To claim your free month visit:

www.forgottenbooks.com/free425847

ISBN 978-0-265-36113-9
PIBN 10425847

By GERALD STANLEY LEE

THE LOST ART OF READING
Mount Tom Edition
New Edition in Two Volumes

I. The Child and the Book :
A Manual for Parents and for Teachers in
Schools and Colleges

II. The Lost Art of Reading ;
or, THE MAN AND THE BOOK

Two Volumes, 8vo.   Sold separately.   Each, net.

G. P. PUTNAM'S SONS
NEW YORK   LONDON

Mount Tom Edition

The Child and The Book

(Reprinted from " The Lost Art of Reading ")

A Manual for Parents, and for Teachers in Schools and Colleges

By

Gerald Stanley Lee

Author of " The Lost Art of Reading," " The Shadow Christ," and " The Voice of the Machines," etc.

G. P. Putnam's Sons

New York and London

The Knickerbocker Press

1907

A213734

To
JENNETTE LEE

A Note

IT has been thought best to accommodate a special demand for certain parts of THE LOST ART OF READING by dividing the book and publishing an edition in two volumes, to be called the MOUNT TOM edition.

The first volume is called THE CHILD AND THE BOOK, and deals with the practical problems of reading, among children and young people, and in schools and colleges, and the second is called THE LOST ART OF READING, or, THE MAN AND THE BOOK, and deals with the more personal and private experiences of the adult reader in his struggle to remain intelligent in modern life.

GERALD STANLEY LEE.

MOUNT TOM,

 NORTHAMPTON MASSACHUSETTS,

September, 1906.

Contents

PART ONE

INTERFERENCES WITH THE READING HABIT

THE DISGRACE OF THE IMAGINATION

PAGE

I—On Wondering Why One Was Born . 3

II—The Top of the Bureau Principle . . 10

THE UNPOPULARITY OF THE FIRST PERSON SINGULAR

I—The First Person a Necessary Evil . . 18

II—The Art of Being Anonymous . . 25

III—Egoism and Society 32

IV—i + I = We 35

V—The Autobiography of Beauty . . 40

THE HABIT OF NOT LETTING ONE'S SELF GO

I—The Country Boy in Literature . . 45

II—The Subconscious Self . . . 51

III—The Organic Principle of Inspiration . 56

**Interfer-
ences with
the reading
habit**

THE HABIT OF ANALYSIS

PAGE

I—If Shakespeare Came to Chicago' . . 6r

II—Analysis Analyzed 72

LITERARY DRILL IN COLLEGE

I—Seeds and Blossoms 80

II—Private Road : Dangerous . . . 86

III—The Organs of Literature . . . 95

IV—Entrance Examinations in Joy . . 100

V—Natural Selection in Theory . . . 107

VI—Natural Selection in Practice . . . 111

VII—The Emancipation of the Teacher . . 118

VIII—The Test of Culture 122

IX—Summary 124

X—A Note 130

PART TWO

POSSIBILITIES

**Possibili-
ties**

I—The Issue 135

II—The First Selection 138

III—Conveniences 139

IV—The Charter of Possibility . . . 146

V—The Great Game 149

VI—Outward Bound 155

Part I

Interferences with the Reading Habit

The First Interference: The Disgrace of the Imagination

I

On Wondering Why One Was Born

THE real trouble with most of the attempts that teachers and parents make, to teach children a vital relation to books, is that they do not believe in the books and that they do not believe in the children.

It is almost impossible to find a child who, in one direction or another, the first few years of his life, is not creative. It is almost impossible to find a parent or a teacher who does not discourage this creativeness. The discouragement begins in a small way, at first, in the

average family, but as the more creative a
child becomes the more inconvenient he is, as
a general rule, every time a boy is caught
being creative, something has to be done to him
about it.

It is a part of the nature of creativeness that
it involves being creative a large part of the
time in the wrong direction. Half-proud and
half-stupefied parents, failing to see that the
mischief in a boy is the entire basis of his education, the mainspring of his life, not being
able to break the mainspring themselves, fre-
quently hire teachers to help them. The
teacher who can break a mainspring first and
keep it from getting mended, is often the most
esteemed in the community. Those who have
broken the most, " secure results." The spectacle of the mechanical, barren, conventional
society so common in the present day, to all
who love their kind is a sign there is no with-
standing. It is a spectacle we can only stand
and watch — some of us,— the huge, dreary
kinetoscope of it, grinding its cogs and wheels,
and swinging its weary faces past our eyes.
The most common sight in it and the one that
hurts the hardest, is the boy who could be
made into a man out of the parts of him that
his parents and teachers are trying to throw
away. The faults of the average child, as
things are going just now, would be the making
of him, if he could be placed in seeing hands.
It may not be possible to educate a boy by

using what has been left out of him, but it is more than possible to begin his education by using what ought to have been left out of him.

So long as parents and teachers are either too dull or too busy to experiment with mischief, to be willing to pay for a child's originality what originality costs, only the most hopeless children can be expected to amount to anything. If we fail to see that originality is worth paying for, that the risk involved in a child's not being creative is infinitely more serious than the risk involved in his being creative in the wrong direction, there is little either for us or for our children to hope for, as the years go on, except to grow duller together. We do not like this growing duller together very well, perhaps, but we have the feeling at least that we have been educated, and when our children become at last as little interested in the workings of their minds, as parents and teachers are in theirs, we have the feeling that they also have been educated. We are not unwilling to admit, in a somewhat useless, kindly, generalising fashion, that vital and beautiful children delight in things, in proportion as they discover them, or are allowed to make them up, but we do not propose in the meantime to have our own children any more vital and beautiful than we can help. In four or five years they discover that a home is a place where the more one thinks of things, the more unhappy he is. In four or five years more they learn that a school is a place where children are expected not to use their brains while they are being cultivated. As long as he is at his mother's breast the typical American child finds that he is admired for thinking of things. When he runs around the house he finds gradually that he is admired very much less for thinking of things. At school he is disciplined for it. In a library, if he has an uncommonly active mind, and takes the liberty of being as alive there, as he is outdoors, if he roams through the books, vaults over their fences, climbs up their mountains, and eats of their fruit, and dreams by their streams, or is caught camping out in their woods, he is made an example of. He is treated as a tramp and an idler, and if he cannot be held down with a dictionary he is looked upon as not worth educating. If his parents decide he shall be educated anyway, dead or alive, or in spite of his being alive, the more he is educated the more he wonders why he was born and the more his teachers from behind their dictionaries, and the other boys from underneath their dictionaries, wonder why he was born. While it may be a general principle that the longer a boy wonders why he was born in conditions like these, and the longer his teachers and parents wonder, the more there is of him, it may be observed that a general principle is not of very much comfort to the boy while the process of wondering is going on. There seems to be no escape from the process, and if, while he is being educated, he is not allowed to use himself, he can hardly be blamed for spending a good deal of his time in wondering why he is not some one else. In a half-seeing, half-blinded fashion he struggles on. If he is obstinate enough, he manages to struggle through with his eyes shut. Sometimes he belongs to a higher kind, and opens his eyes and struggles.

With the average boy the struggle with the School and the Church is less vigorous than the struggle at home. It is more hopeless. A mother is a comparatively simple affair. One can either manage a mother or be managed. It is merely a matter of time. It is soon settled. There is something there. She is not boundless, intangible. The School and the Church are different. With the first fresh breaths of the world tingling in him, the youth stands before them. They are entirely new to him. They are huge, immeasurable, unaccountable. They loom over him—a part of the structure of the universe itself. A mother can meet one in a door. The problem is concentrated. The Church stretches beyond the sunrise. The School is part of the horizon of the earth, and what after all is his own life and who is he that he should take account of it? Out of space—out of time—out of history they come to him—the Church and the School. They are the assembling of all mankind around

On
Wonder=
ing Why
One Was
Born

his soul. Each with its Cone of Ether, its desire to control the breath of his life, its determination to do his breathing for him, to push the Cone down over him, looms above him and above all in sight, before he speaks— before he is able to speak.

It is soon over. He lies passive and insensible at last,—as convenient as though he were dead, and the Church and the School operate upon him. They remove as many of his natural organs as they can, put in Presbyterian ones perhaps, or School-Board ones instead. Those that cannot be removed are numbed. When the time is fulfilled and the youth is cured of enough life at last to like living with the dead, and when it is thought he is enough like every one else to do, he is given his degree and sewed up.

After the sewing up his history is better imagined than described. Not being interesting to himself, he is not apt to be very interesting to any one else, and because of his lack of interest in himself he is called the average man.*

---

* A Typical Case: " The brain was cut away neatly and dressed. A healthy yearling calf was tied down, her skull cut away, and a lobe of brain removed and fitted into the cavity in L's head. The wound was dressed and trephined, and the results awaited. The calf's head was fixed up with half a brain in it. Both the man and the calf have progressed satisfactorily, and the man is nearly as well as before the operation." —Daily Paper.

The main distinction of every greater or more extraordinary book is that it has been written by an extraordinary man—a natural or wild man, a man of genius, who has never been operated on. The main distinction of the man of talent is that he has somehow managed to escape a complete operation. It is a matter of common observation in reading biography that in proportion as men have had lasting power in the world there has been something irregular in their education. These irregularities, whether they happen to be due to overwhelming circumstance or to overwhelming temperament, seem to sum themselves up in one fundamental and comprehensive irregularity that penetrates them all—namely, every powerful mind, in proportion to its power, either in school or out of it or in spite of it, has educated itself. The ability that many men have used to avoid being educated is exactly the same ability they have used afterward to move the world with. In proportion as they have moved the world, they are found to have kept the lead in their education from their earliest years, to have had a habit of initiative as well as hospitality, to have maintained a creative, selective, active attitude toward all persons and toward all books that have been brought within range of their lives.

II

The Top of the Bureau Principle

The experience of being robbed of a story we are about to read, by the good friend who cannot help telling how it comes out, is an occasional experience in the lives of older people, but it sums up the main sensation of life in the career of a child. The whole existence of a boy may be said to be a daily—almost hourly—struggle to escape from being told things.

It has been found that the best way to emphasise a fact in the mind of a bright boy is to discover some way of not saying anything about it. And this is not because human nature is obstinate, but because facts have been intended from the beginning of the world to speak for themselves, and to speak better than any one can speak for them. When a fact speaks, God speaks. Considering the way that most persons who are talking about the truth see fit to rush in and interrupt Him, the wonder is not that children grow less and less interested in truth as they grow older, but that they are interested in truth at all—even lies about the truth.

The real trouble with most men and women as parents is, that they have had to begin life with parents of their own. When the child's first memory of God is a father or mother interrupting Him, he is apt to be under the impression, when he grows up, that God can only be introduced to his own children by never being allowed to get a word in. If we as much as see a Fact coming toward a child—most of us—we either run out where the child is, and bring him into the house and cry over him, or we rush to his side and look anxious and stand in front of the Fact, and talk to him about it.

And yet it is doubtful if there has ever been a boy as yet worth mentioning, who did not wish we would stand a little more one side—let him have it out with things. He is very weary—if he really amounts to anything—of having everything about him prepared for him. There has never been a live boy who would not throw a store-plaything away in two or three hours for a comparatively imperfect plaything he had made himself. He is equally indifferent to a store Fact, and a boy who does not see through a store-God, or a store-book, or a store-education sooner than ninety-nine parents out of a hundred and sooner than most synods, is not worth bringing up.

No just or comprehensive principle can be found to govern the reading of books that cannot be made to apply, by one who really believes it (though in varying degrees), to the genius and to the dolt. It is a matter of history that a boy of fine creative powers can only be taught a true relation to books through

an appeal to his own discoveries; but what is
being especially contended for, and what most
needs to be emphasised in current education,
is the fact that the boy of ordinary creative
powers can only be taught to read in the same
way—by a slower, broader, and more patient
appeal to his own discoveries. The boy of no
creative powers whatever, if he is ever born,
should not be taught to read at all. Creation
is the essence of knowing, and teaching him
to read merely teaches him more ways of not
knowing. It gives him a wider range of places
to be a nobody in—takes away his last opportunity for thinking of anything—that is, getting the meaning of anything for himself. If
a man's heart does not beat for him, why sub-
stitute a hot-water bottle? The less a mind
is able to do, the less it can afford to have anything done for it. It will be a great day for
education when we all have learned that the
genius and the dolt can only be educated—at
different rates of speed—in exactly the same
way. The trouble with our education now is,
that many of us do not see that a boy who has
been presented with an imitation brain is a
deal worse off than a boy who, in spite of his
teachers, has managed to save his real one,
and has not used it yet.

It is dangerous to give a program for a principle to those who do not believe in the
principle, and who do not believe in it instinctively, but if a program were to be given it

would be something like this: It would assume that the best way to do with an uncreative mind is to put the owner of it where his mind will be obliged to create.

First. Decide what the owner of the mind most wants in the world.

Second. Put this thing, whatever it may be, where the owner of the mind cannot get it unless he uses his mind. Take pains to put it where he can get it, if he does use his mind.

Third. Lure him on. It is education.

If this principle is properly applied to books, there is not a human being living on the earth who will not find himself capable of reading books—as far as he goes—with his whole mind and his whole body. He will read a printed page as eagerly as he lives, and he will read it in exactly the same way that he lives—with his imagination. A boy lives with his imagination every hour of his life—except in school. The moment he discovers, or is allowed to discover, that reading a book and living a day are very much alike, that they are both parts of the same act, and that they are both properly done in the same way, he will drink up knowledge as Job did scorning, like water.

But it is objected that many children are entirely imitative, and that the imagination cannot be appealed to with them and that they cut themselves off from creativeness at every point.

While it is inevitable in the nature of things

that many children should be largely imitative, there is not a child that does not do some of his imitating in a creative way, give the hint to his teachers even in his imitations, of where his creativeness would come if it were allowed to. His very blunders in imitating, point to desires that would make him creative of them-selves, if followed up. Some children have many desires in behalf of which they become creative. Others are creative only in behalf of a few. But there is always a single desire in a child's nature through which his creative-ness can be called out.

A boy learns to live, to command his body, through the desires which make him creative with it—hunger, and movement, and sleep—desires the very vegetables are stirred with, and the boy who does not find himself respond-ing to them, who can help responding to them, does not exist. There may be times when a boy has no desire to fill himself with food, and when he has no desire to think, but if he is kept hungry he is soon found doing both—thinking things into his stomach. A stomach, in the average boy, will all but take the part of a brain itself, for the time being, to avoid being empty. If a human being is alive at all, there is always at least one desire he can be educated with, prodded into creativeness, until he learns the habit and the pleasure of it. The best qualification for a nurse for a child whose creativeness turns on his stomach, is a natural gift for keeping food on the tops of bureaus and shelves just out of reach. The best qualification for a teacher is infinite contrivance in high bureaus. The applying of the Top of the High Bureau to all knowledge and to all books is what true education is for.

It is generally considered a dangerous thing to do, to turn a child loose in a library. It might fairly be called a dangerous thing to do if it were not much more dangerous not to. The same forces that wrought themselves into the books when they were being made can be trusted to gather and play across them on the shelves. These forces are the self-propelling and self-healing forces of the creative mood. The creative mood protects the books, and it protects all who come near the books. It protects from the inside. It toughens and makes supple. Parents who cannot trust a boy to face the weather in a library should never let him outdoors.

Trusting a boy to the weather in a library may have its momentary embarrassments, but it is immeasurably the shortest and most natural way to bring him into a vital connection with books. The first condition of a vital connection with books is that he shall make the connection for himself. The relation will be vital in proportion as he makes it himself.

The fact that he will begin to use his five reading senses by trying to connect in the wrong way, or by connecting with the wrong books or parts of books, is a reason, not for action on the part of parents and teachers, but for inspired waiting. As a vital relation to books is the most immeasurable outfit for living and the most perfect protection against the dangers of life, a boy can have, the one point to be borne in mind is not the book but the boy—the instinct of curiosity in the boy.

A boy who has all his good discoveries in books made for him—spoiled for him, if he has any good material in him—will proceed to make bad ones. The vices would be nearly as safe from interference as the virtues, if they were faithfully cultivated in Sunday-schools or by average teachers in day-schools. Sin itself is uninteresting when one knows all about it. The interest of the average young man in many a more important sin to-day is only kept up by the fact that no one stands by with a book teaching him how to do it. Whatever the expression "original sin" may have meant in the first place, it means now that we are full of original sin because we are not given a chance to be original in anything else. A virtue may be defined as an act so good that a religiously trained youth cannot possibly learn anything more about it. A classic is a pleasure hurried into a responsibility, a book read by every man before he has anything to read it with. A classical author is a man who, if he could look ahead—could see the generations standing in rows to read his book, toeing the line to love it—would not read it himself.

Any training in the use of books that does not base its whole method of rousing the instinct of curiosity, and keeping it aroused, is a wholesale slaughter, not only of the minds that might live in the books, but of the books themselves. To ignore the central curiosity of a child's life, his natural power of self-discovery in books, is to dispense with the force of gravity in books, instead of taking advantage of it.

The Second Interference: The Unpopularity of the First Person Singular

I

The First Person a Necessary Evil

GREAT emphasis is being laid at the present time upon the tools that readers ought to have to do their reading with. We seem to be living in a reference-book age. Whatever else may be claimed for our own special generation it stands out as having one inspiration that is quite its own—the inspiration of conveniences. That these conveniences have their place, that one ought to have the best of them there can be no doubt, but it is very important to bear in mind, particularly in the present public mood, that if one cannot have all of these conveniences, or even the best of them, the one absolutely necessary reference book in reading the masters of literature is one that every man has.

It is something of a commonplace—a rather modest volume with most of us, summed up on a tombstone generally, easily enough, but we are bound to believe after all is said and done that the great masterpiece among reference books, for every man,—the one originally intended by the Creator for every man to use,—is the reference book of his own life. We believe that the one direct and necessary thing for a man to do, if he is going to be a good reader, is to make this reference book—his own private edition of it—as large and complete as possible. Everything refers to it, whatever his reading is. Shakespeare and the New York *World*, Homer and *Harper's Bazar*, Victor Hugo and *The Forum*, *Babyhood* and the Bible all refer to it,—are all alike in making their references (when they are really looked up) to private editions. Other editions do not work. In proportion as they are powerful in modern life, all the books and papers that we have are engaged in the business of going about the world discovering people to themselves, unroofing first person singulars in it, getting people to use their own reference books on all life. Literature is a kind of vast international industry of comparing life. We read to look up references in our own souls. The immortality of Homer and the circulation of the *Ladies' Home Journal* both conform to this fact, and it is equally the secret of the last page of *Harper's Bazar* and of Hamlet and of the grave and monthly lunge of *The Forum* at passing events. The difference of appeal may be as wide as the east and the west, but the east and the west are in human nature and not in the nature of the appeal. The larger selves look themselves up in the greater writers and the smaller selves spell themselves out in the smaller ones. It is here we all behold as in some vast reflection or mirage of the reading world our own souls crowding and jostling, little and great, against the walls of their years, seeking to be let out, to look out, to look over, to look up—that they may find their possible selves.

When men are allowed to follow what might be called the forces of nature in the reading world they are seen to read:

1st. About themselves.

2nd. About people they know.

3rd. About people they want to know.

4th. God.

Next to their interest in persons is their interest in things:

1st. Things that they have themselves.

2nd. Things that people they know, have.

3rd. Things they want to have.

4th. Things they ought to want to have.

5th. Other things.

6th. The universe—things God has.

7th. God.

A scale like this may not be very complimentary to human nature. Some of us feel that it is appropriate and possibly a little religious to think that it is not. But the scale is here. It is mere psychological-matter-of-fact. It is the way things are made, and while it may not be quite complimentary to human nature, it seems to be more complimentary to God to believe, in spite of appearauces, that this scale from I to God is made right and should be used as it stands. It seems to have been in general use among our more considerable men in the world and among all our great men and among all who have made others great. They do not seem to have been ashamed of it. They have climbed up frankly on it—most of them, in full sight of all men—from I to God. They have claimed that everybody (including themselves) was identified with God, and they have made people believe it. It is the few in every generation who have dared to believe in this scale, and who have used it, who have been the leaders of the rest. The measure of a man's being seems to be the swiftness with which his nature runs from the bottom of this scale to the top, the swiftness with which he identifies himself, says " I " in all of it. The measure of his ability to read on any particular subject is the swiftness with which he runs the scale from the bottom to the top on that subject, makes the trip with his soul from his own little I to God. When he has mastered the subject, he makes the run almost without knowing it, sees it as it is, *i. e.*, identifies himself with God on it. The principle is one which reaches under all mastery in the world, from the art of prophecy even to the art of politeness. The man who makes the trip on any subject from the first person out through the second person, to the farthest bounds of the third person,—that is, who identifies himself with all men's lives, is called the poet or seer, the master-lover of persons. The man who makes the trip most swiftly from his own things to other men's things and to God's things—the Universe—is called the scientist, the master-lover of things. The God is he who identifies his own personal life with all lives and his own things with all men's things—who says " I " forever everywhere.

The reason that the Hebrew Bible has had more influence in history than all other literatures combined, is that there are fewer emasculated men in it. The one really fundamental and astonishing thing about the Bible is the way that people have of talking about themselves in it. No other nation that has ever existed on the earth would ever have thought of daring to publish a book like the Bible. So far as the plot is concerned, the fundamental literary conception, it is all the Bible comes to

practically—two or three thousand years of it
—a long row of people talking about themselves. The Hebrew nation has been the
leading power in history because the Hebrew
man, in spite of all his faults has always had
the feeling that God sympathised with him, in
being interested in himself. He has dared to
feel identified with God. It is the same in all
ages—not an age but one sees a Hebrew in it,
out under his lonely heaven standing and crying "God and I." It is the one great spectacle
of the Soul this little world has seen. Are not
the mightiest faces that come to us flickering
out of the dark, their faces? Who can look at
the past who does not see—who does not always
see—some mighty Hebrew in it singing and
struggling with God? What is it—what else
could it possibly be but the Hebrew soul, like
a kind of pageantry down the years between us
and God, that would ever have made us guess—
men of the other nations—that a God belonged
to us, or that a God could belong to us and be a
God at all? Have not all the other races, each
in their turn spawning in the sun and lost in
the night, vanished because they could not say
" I " before God? The nations that are left,
the great nations of the modern world, are but
the moral passengers of the Hebrews, hangers-
on to the race that can say " I "—I to the nth
power,—the race that has dared to identify itself
with God. The fact that the Hebrew, instead
of saying God and I, has turned it around

sometimes and said I and God is neither here nor there in the end.   It is because the Hebrew has kept to the main point, has felt related to God (the main point a God cares about), that he has been the most heroic and athletic figure in human history—comes nearer to the God-size.   The rest of the nations sitting about and wondering in the dark, have called this thing in the Hebrew " religious genius."   If one were to try to sum up what religious genius is, in the Hebrew, or to account for the spiritual and material supremacy of the Hebrew in history, in a single fact, it would be the fact that Moses, their first great leader, when he wanted to say " It seems to me," said " The Lord said unto Moses."

The Hebrews may have written a book that teaches, of all others, self-renunciation, but the way they taught it was self-assertion.   The Bible begins with a meek Moses who teaches by saying " The Lord said unto Moses," and it comes to its climax in a lowly and radiant man who dies on a cross to say " I and the Father are one."   The man Jesus seems to have called himself God because he had a divine habit of identifying himself, because he had kept on identifying himself with others until the first person and the second person and the third person were as one to him.   The distinction of the New Testament is that it is the one book the world has seen, which dispenses with pronouns.   It is a book that sums up pronouns and numbers, singular and plural, first person, second and third person, and all, in the one great central pronoun of the universe. The very stars speak it—WE.

We is a developed I.

The first person may not be what it ought to be either as a philosophy or an experience, but it has been considered good enough to make Bibles out of, and it does seem as if a good word might occasionally be said for it in modern times, as if some one ought to be born before long, who will give it a certain standing, a certain moral respectability once more in human life and in the education of human life.

It would not seem to be an overstatement that the best possible book to give a child to read at any time is the one that makes the most cross references at that time to his undeveloped We.

II

The Art of Being Anonymous

The main difficulty in getting a child to live in the whole of his nature, to run the scale from the bottom to the top, from " I " to God, is to persuade his parents and teachers, and the people who crowd around him to educate him, that he must begin at the bottom.

The Unpopularity of the First Person Singular in current education naturally follows from

The Disgrace of the Imagination in it. Our typical school is not satisfied with cutting off a boy's imagination about the outer world that lies around him. It amputates his imagination at its tap root. It stops a boy's imagination about himself, and the issues, connections, and possibilities of his own life.

Inasmuch as the education of a child—his relation to books—must be conducted either with reference to evading personality, or accumulating it, the issue is one that must be squarely drawn from the first. Beginning at the bottom is found by society at large to be such an inconvenient and painstaking process, that the children who are allowed to lay a foundation for personality—to say " I " in its disagreeable stages—seem to be confined, for the most part, to either one or the other of two classes — the Incurable or the Callous. The more thorough a child's nature is, the more real his processes are, the more incurable he is bound to be—secretly if he is sensitive, and offensively if he is callous. In either case the fact is the same. The child unconsciously acts on the principle that self-assertion is self-preservation. One of the first things that he discovers is that self-preservation is the last thing polite parents desire in a child. If he is to be preserved, they will preserve him themselves.

The conspiracy begins in the earliest days. The world rolls over him. The home and the church and the school and the printed book

roll over him. The story is the same in all.
Education—originally conceived as drawing a
boy out — becomes a huge, elaborate, overwhelming scheme for squeezing him in—for
keeping him squeezed in. He is mobbed on
every side. At school the teachers crowd
round him and say " I " for him. At home
his parents say " I " for him. At church the
preacher says " I " for him. And when he re-
treats into the privacy of his own soul and be-
takes himself to a book, the book is a classic
and the book says " I " for him. When he
says " I " himself after a few appropriate years,
he says it in disguised quotation marks. If he
cannot always avoid it—if in some unguarded
moment he is particularly alive about something and the " I " comes out on it, society
expects him to be ashamed of it, at least to
avoid the appearance of not being ashamed of
it. If he writes he is desired to say " we."
Sometimes he shades himself off into " the
present writer." Sometimes he capitulates in
bare initials.

There are very few people who do not live
in quotation marks most of their lives. They
would die in them and go to heaven in them,
if they could. Nine times out of ten it is
some one else's heaven they want to go to.
The number of people who would know what
to do or how to act in this world or the next,
without their quotation marks on, is getting
more limited every year.

And yet one could not very well imagine a world more prostrate that this one is, before a man without quotation marks. It dotes on personality. It spends hundreds of years at a time in yearning for a great man. But it wants its great man finished. It is never willing to pay what he costs. It is particularly unwilling to pay what he costs as it goes along. The great man as a boy has had to pay for himself. The bare feat of keeping out of quotation marks has cost him generally more than he thought he was worth—and has had to be paid in advance.

There is a certain sense in which it is true that every boy, at least at the point where he is especially alive, is a kind of great man in miniature—has the same experience, that is, in growing. Many a boy who has been regularly represented to himself as a monster, a curiosity of selfishness (and who has believed it), has had occasion to observe when he grew up that some of his selfishness was real selfishness and that some of it was life. The things he was selfish with, he finds as he grows older, are the things he has been making a man out of. As a boy, however, he does not get much inkling of this. He finds he is being brought up in a world where boys who so little know how to play with their things that they give them away, are pointed out to him as generous, and where boys who are so bored with their own minds that they prefer other people's, are considered modest. If he knew in the days when models are being pointed out to him, that the time would soon come in the world for boys like these when it would make little difference either to the boys themselves, or to any one·else, whether they were generous or modest or not, it would make his education happier. In the meantime, in his disgrace, he does not guess what a good example to models he is. Very few other people guess it.

The general truth, that when a man has nothing to be generous with, and nothing to be modest about, even his virtues are super-fluous, is realised by society at large in a pleasant helpless fashion in its bearing on the man, but its bearing on the next man, on education, on the problem of human development, is almost totally overlooked.

The youth who grasps at everything in sight to have his experience with it, who cares more for the thing than he does for the person it comes from, and more for his experience with the thing than he does for the thing, is by no means an inspiring spectacle while this process is going on, and he is naturally in perpetual disgrace, but in proportion as they are wise, our best educators are aware that in all probability this same youth will wield more spiritual power in the world, and do more good in it, than nine or ten pleasantly smoothed and adjustable persons. His boy-faults are his man-virtues wrongside out.

There are very few lives of powerful men in modern times that do not illustrate this. The men who do not believe it—who do not approve of illustrating it, have illustrated it the most—devoted their lives to it. It would be hard to find a man of any special importance in modern biography who has not been indebted to the sins of his youth. "It is the things I ought not to have done—see page 93, 179, 321," says the average autobiography, "which have been the making of me." "They were all good things for me to do (see page 526, 632, 720), but I did not think so when I did them. Neither did any one else." "Studying Shakespeare and the theatre in the theological seminary, and taking walks instead of examinations in college," says the biography of Beecher (between the lines), "meant definite moral degeneration to me. I did habitually what I could not justify at the time, either to myself or to others, and I have had to make up since for all the moral degeneration, item by item, but the things I got with the degeneration when I got it—habits of imagination, and expression, headway of personality—are the things that have given me all my inspirations for being moral since." "What love of liberty I have," Wendell Phillips seems to say, "I got from loving my own." It is the boy who loves his liberty so much that he insists on having it to do wrong with, as well as right, who in the long run gets the most right done. The basis of character is moral experiment and almost all the men who have discovered different or beautiful or right habits of life for men, have discovered them by doing wrong long enough. (The ice is thin at this point, Gentle Reader, for many of us, perhaps, but it has held up our betters.) The fact of the matter seems to be that a man's conscience in this world, especially if it is an educated one, or borrowed from his parents, can get as much in his way as anything else. There is no doubt that The Great Spirit prefers to lead a man by his conscience, but if it cannot be done, if a man's conscience has no conveniences for being led, He leads him against his conscience. The doctrine runs along the edge of a precipice (like all the best ones), but if there is one gift rather than another to be prayed for in this world it is the ability to recognise the crucial moment that sometimes comes in a human life — the moment when The Almighty Himself gets a man — against his conscience — to do right. It seems to be the way that some consciences are meant to grow, by trying wrong things on a little. Thousands of inferior people can be seen every day stumbling over their sins to heaven, while the rest of us are holding back with our virtues. It has been intimated from time to time in this world that all men are sinners. Inasmuch as things are arranged so that men can sin in doing right things, and sin in doing wrong ones both, they can hardly miss it. The real religion of every age seems to have looked a little askance at perfection, even at purity, has gone its way in a kind of fine straightforwardness, has spent itself in an inspired blundering, in progressive noble culminating moral experiment.

The basis for a great character seems to be the capacity for intense experience with the character one already has. So far as most of us can judge, experience, in proportion as it has been conclusive and economical, has had to be (literally or with one's imagination) in the first person. The world has never really wanted yet (in spite of appearances) its own way with a man. It wants the man. It is what he is that concerns it. All that it asks of him, and all that he has to give, is the surplus of himself. The trouble with our modern fashion of substituting the second person or the third person for the first, in a man's education, is that it takes his capacity for intense experience of himself, his chance for having a surplus of himself, entirely away.

III

Egoism and Society

That the unpopularity of the first person singular is honestly acquired and heartily deserved, it would be useless to deny. Every one who has ever had a first person singular for a longer or shorter period in his life knows that it is a disagreeable thing and that every one else knows it, in nine cases out of ten, at least, and about nine tenths of the time during its development. The fundamental question does not concern itself with the first person singular being agreeable or disagreeable, but with what to do with it, it being the necessary evil that it is.

It seems to be a reasonable position that what should be objected to in the interests of society, is not egoism, a man's being interested in himself, but the lack of egoism, a man's having a self that does not include others. The trouble would seem to be—not that people use their own private special monosyllable overmuch, but that there is not enough of it, that nine times out of ten, when they write " I " it should be written " i."

In the face of the political objection, the objection of the State to the first person singular, the egoist defends every man's reading for himself as follows. Any book that is allowed to come between a man and himself is doing him and all who know him a public injury. The most important and interesting fact about a man, to other people, is his attitude toward himself. It determines his attitude toward every one else. The most fundamental question of every State is: " What is each man's attitude in this State toward himself? What can it be?'' A man's expectancy toward himself, so far as the State is concerned, is the moral centre of citizenship. It determines how much of what he expects he will expect of himself, and how much he will expect of others and how much of books. The man who expects too much of himself develops into the headlong and dangerous citizen who threatens society with his strength — goes elbowing about in it — insisting upon living other people's lives for them as well as his own. The man who expects too much of others threatens society with weariness. He is always expecting other people to do his living for him. The man who expects too much of books lives neither in himself nor in any one else. The career of the Paper Doll is open to him. History seems to be always taking turns with these three temperaments whether in art or religion or public affairs,—the over-manned, the under-manned, and the over-read — the Tyrant, the Tramp, and the Paper Doll. Between the man who keeps things in his own hands, and the man who does not care to, and the man who has no hands, the State has a hard time. Nothing could be more important to the existence of the State than that every man in it shall expect just enough of himself and just enough of others and just enough of the world of books. Living is adjusting these worlds to one another. The central fact about society is the way it helps a man with himself.

The society which cuts a man off from himself cuts him still farther off from every one else. A man's reading in the first person—enough to have a first person—enough to be identified with himself, is one of the defences of society.

IV

𝔦 + 𝔫 = 𝔚𝔢

The most natural course for a human being, who is going to identify himself with other people, is to begin by practising on himself. If he has not succeeded in identifying himself with himself, he makes very trying work of the rest of us. A man who has not learned to say "I" and mean something very real by it, has it not in his power, without dulness or impertinence, to say "you" to any living creature. If a man has not learned to say "you," if he has not taken hold of himself, interpreted and adjusted himself to those who are face to face with him, the wider and more general privilege of saying "they," of judging any part of mankind or any temperament in it, should be kept away from him. It is only as one has experienced a temperament, has in some mood of one's life said "I" in that temperament, that one has the outfit for passing an opinion on it, or the outfit for living with it, or for being in the same world with it.

There are times, it must be confessed, when

{+1=We

Christ's command, that every man shall love his neighbour as himself, seems inconsiderate. There are some of us who cannot help feeling, when we see a man coming along toward us proposing to love us a little while the way he loves himself, that our permission might have been asked. If there is one inconvenience rather than another in our modern Christian society, it is the general unprotected sense one has in it, the number of people there are about in it (let loose by Sunday-school teachers and others) who are allowed to go around loving other people the way they love themselves. A codicil or at least an explanatory footnote to the Golden Rule, in the general interest of neighbours, would be widely appreciated. How shall a man dare to love his neighbour as him-self, until he loves himself, has a self that he really loves, a self he can really love, and loves it? There is no more sad or constant spectacle that this modern world has to face than the spectacle of the man who has over-looked himself, bustling about in it, trying to give honour to other people,—the man who has never been able to help himself, hurrying anxious to and fro as if he could help some one else.

It is not too much to say "Charity begins at home." Everything does. The one person who has the necessary training for being an altruist is the alert egoist who does not know he is an altruist. His service to society is a more intense and comprehensive selfishness. He would be cutting acquaintance with himself not to render it. When he says "I" he means "we," and the second and third persons are grown dim to him.

An absolutely perfect virtue is the conveying of a man's self, with a truth, to others. The virtues that do not convey anything are cheap and common enough. Favours can be had almost any day from anybody, if one is not too particular, and so can blank staring self-sacrifices. One feels like putting up a sign over the door of one's life, with some people: "Let no man do me a favour except he do it as a self-indulgence." Even kindness wears out, shows through, becomes impertinent, if it is not a part of selfishness. It may be that there are certain rudimentary virtues the outer form of which had better be maintained in the world, whether they can be maintained spiritually— that is, thoroughly and egotistically, or not. If my enemy who lives under the hill will continne to not-murder me, I desire him to continne whether he enjoys not-murdering me or not. But it is no credit to him. Except in some baldly negative fashion as this, however, it is literally true that a man's virtues are of little account to others except as they are of account to him, and except he enjoys them as much as his vices. The first really important shock that comes to a young man's religious sentiment in this world is the number of

i + 1 = We

bored-looking people around, doing right.
An absolutely substantial and perfect love
is transfigured selfishness. It is no mere
playing with words to say this, nor is it
substituting a comfortable and pleasant doctrine for a strenuous altruism. If it were as
light and graceful an undertaking to have
enough selfishness to go around, to live in the
whole of a universe like this, as it is to slip out
of even living in one's self in it, like a mere
shadow or altruist, egoism were superficial
enough. As it is, egoism being terribly or
beautifully alive, so far as it goes, is now and
always has been, and always must be the running gear of the spiritual world—egoism social-
ised. The first person is what the second and
third persons are made out of. Altruism, as
opposed to egoism, except in a temporary
sense, is a contradiction in terms. Unless a
man has a life to identify other lives with, a
self which is the symbol through which he
loves all other selves and all other experiences,
he is selfish in the true sense.

With all our Galileos, Agassizes, and Shake-
speares, the universe has not grown in its
countless centuries. It has not been getting
higher and wider over us since the human
race began. It is not a larger universe. It is
lived in by larger men, more all-absorbing, all-
identifying, and selfish men. It is a universe
in which a human being is duly born, given
place with such a self as he happens to have,

and he is expected to grow up to it. Barring a certain amount of wear and tear and a few minor rearrangements on the outside, it is the same universe that it was in the beginning, and is now and always will be quite the same universe, whether a man grows up to it or not. The larger universe is not one that comes with the telescope. It comes with the larger self, the self that by reaching farther and farther in, reaches farther and farther out. It is as if the sky were a splendour that grew by night out of his own heart, the tent of his love of God spreading its roof over the nature of things. The greater distance knowledge reaches, the more it has to be personal, because it has to be spiritual.

The one thing that it is necessary to do in any part of the world to make any branch of knowledge or deed of mercy, a living and eager thing, is to get men to see how direct its bearing is upon themselves. The man who does not feel concerned when the Armenians are massacred, thousands of miles away, because there is a sea between, is not a different man in kind from the man who does feel concerned. The difference is one of degree. It is a matter of area in living. The man who does feel concerned has a larger self. He sees further, feels the cry as the cry of his own children. He has learned the oneness and is touched with the closeness, of the great family of the world.

V

The Autobiography of Beauty

But the brunt of the penalty of the unpopularity of the first person singular in modern society falls upon the individual. The hard part of it, for a man who has not the daily habit of being a companion to himself, is his own personal private sense of emptiness—of missing things. All the universe gets itself addressed to some one else — a great showy heartless pantomime it rolls over him, beckoning with its nights and days and winds and faces—always beckoning, but to some one else. All that seems to be left to him in a universe is a kind of keeping up appearances in it—a looking as if he lived—a hurrying, dishonest trying to forget. He dare not sit down and think. He spends his strength in racing with himself to get away from himself, and those greatest days of all in human life—the days when men grow old, world-gentle, and still and deep before their God, are the days he dreads the most. He can only look forward to old age as the time when a man sits down with his lie at last, and day after day and night after night faces infinite and eternal loneliness in his own heart.

It is the man who cuts acquaintance with himself, who dares to be lonely with himself, who dares the supreme daring in this world.

He and his loneliness are hermetically sealed up together in infinite Time, infinite Space,—not a great man of all that have been, not a star or flower, not even a great book that can get at him.

It is the nature of a great book that in proportion as it is beautiful it makes itself helpless before a human soul. Like music or poetry or painting it lays itself radiant and open before all that lies before it — to everything or to nothing, whatever it may be. It makes the direct appeal. Before the days and years of a man's life it stands. "Is not this so?" it says. It never says less than this. It does not know how to say more.

A bare and trivial book stops with what it says itself. A great book depends now and forever upon what it makes a man say back, and if he does not say anything, if he does not bring anything to it to say, nothing out of his own observation, passion, experience, to be called out by the passing words upon the page, the most living book, in its board and paper prison, is a dead and helpless thing before a Dead Soul. The helplessness of the Dead Soul lies upon it.

Perhaps there is no more important distinction between a great book and a little book than this — that the great book is always a listener before a human life, and the little book takes nothing for granted of a reader. It does not expect anything of him. The littler it is, the less it expects and the more it explains. Nothing that is really great and living explains. Living is enough. If greatness does not explain by being great, nothing smaller can explain it. God never explains. He merely appeals to every man's first person singular. Religion is not what He has told to men. It is what He has made men wonder about until they have been determined to find out. The stars have never been published with footnotes. The sun, with its huge, soft shining on people, kept on with the shining even when the people thought it was doing so trivial and undignified and provincial a thing as to spend its whole time going around them, and around their little earth, that they might have light on it perchance, and be kept warm. The moon has never gone out of its way to prove that it is not made of green cheese. And this present planet we are allowed the use of from year to year, which was so little observed for thousands of generations that all the people on it supposed it was flat, made no answer through the centuries. It kept on burying them one by one, and waited—like a work of genius or a masterpiece.

In proportion as a thing is beautiful, whether of man or God, it has this heroic helplessness about it with the passing soul or generation of souls. If people are foolish, it can but appeal from one dear, pitiful fool to another until enough of us have died to make it time for a wise man again. History is a series of crises like this, in which once in so often men who say " I " have crossed the lives of mortals—have puzzled the world enough to be remembered in it, like Socrates, or been abused by it enough to make it love them forever, like Christ.

The greatest revelation of history is the patience of the beauty in it, and truth can always be known by the fact that it is the only thing in the wide world that can afford to wait. A true book does not go about advertising itself, huckstering for souls, arranging its greatness small enough. It waits. Sometimes for twenty years it waits for us, sometimes for forty, sometimes sixty, and then when the time is fulfilled and we come at length and lay before it the burden of the blind and blundering years we have tried to live, it does little with us, after all, but to bring these same years singing and crying and struggling back to us, that through their shadowy doors we may enter at last the confessional of the human heart, and cry out there, or stammer or whisper or sing there, the prophecy of our own lives. Dead words out of dead dictionaries the book brings to us. It is a great book because it is a listening book, because it makes the unspoken to speak and the dead to live in it. To the vanished pen and the yellowed paper of the man who writes to us, thy soul and mine, Gentle Reader, shall call back, " This is the truth."

If a book has force in it, whatever its literary

form may be, or however disguised, it is biography appealing to biography. If a book has
great force in it, it is autobiography appealing
to autobiography. The great book is always
a confession — a moral adventure with its
reader, an incredible confidence.

The Third Interference: The Habit of Not Letting One's Self Go

I

The Country Boy in Literature

"LET not any Parliament Member," says Carlyle, "ask of the Present Editor 'What is to be done?' Editors are not here to say, 'How.'"

"Which is both ungracious and tantalisingly elusive," suggests a Professor of Literature, who has been recently criticising the Nineteenth Century.

This criticism, as a part of an estimate of Thomas Carlyle, is not only a criticism on itself and an autobiography besides, but it sums up, in a more or less characteristic fashion

perhaps, what might be called the ultra-academic attitude in reading.   The ultra-academic
attitude may be defined as the attitude of sitting down and being told things, and of expecting all other persons to sit down and be
told things, and of judging all authors, principles, men, and methods accordingly.

If the universe were what in most libraries
and clubs to-day it is made to seem, a kind
of infinite Institution of Learning, a Lecture
Room on a larger scale, and if all the men in
it, instead of doing and singing in it, had
spent their days in delivering lectures to it,
there would be every reason, in a universe
arranged for lectures, why we should exact of
those who give them, that they should make
the truth plain to us — so plain that there
would be nothing left for us to do, with truth,
but to read it in the printed book, and then
analyse the best analysis of it—and die.

It seems to be quite generally true of those
who have been the great masters of literature,
however, that in proportion as they have been
great they have proved to be as ungracious
and as tantalisingly elusive as the universe
itself.   They have refused, without exception,
to bear down on the word " how."   They have
almost never told men what to do, and have
confined themselves to saying something that
would make them do it, and make them find
a way to do it.   This something that they
have said, like the something that they have

lived, has come to them they know not how, and it has gone from them they know not how, sometimes not even when. It has been incommunicable, incalculable, infinite, the subconscious self of each of them, the voice beneath the voice, calling down the corridors of the world.

If a boy from the country were to stand in a city street before the window of a shop, gazing into it with open mouth, he would do more in five or six minutes to measure the power and calibre of the passing men and women than almost any device that could be arranged. Ninety-five out of a hundred of them, probably, would smile a superior smile at him and hurry on. Out of the remaining five, four would look again and pity him. One, perhaps, would honour and envy him.

The boy who, in a day like the present one, is still vital enough to forget how he looks in enjoying something, is not only a rare and refreshing spectacle, but he is master of the most important intellectual and moral superiority a boy can be master of, and if, in spite of teachers and surroundings, he can keep this superiority long enough, or until he comes to be a man, he shall be the kind of man whose very faults shall be remembered better and cherished more by a doting world than the virtues of the rest of us.

The most important fact—perhaps the only important fact—about James Boswell—the

country boy of literature—is that, whatever
may have been his limitations, he had the
most important gift that life can give to a man
—the gift of forgetting himself in it.   In the
Fleet Street of letters, smiling at him and jeer-
ing by him, who does not always see James
Boswell, completely lost to the street, gaping
at the soul of Samuel Johnson as if it were the
show window of the world, as if to be allowed
to look at a soul like this were almost to have
a soul one's self?

Boswell's *Life of Johnson* is a classic because
James Boswell had the classic power in him of
unconsciousness.   To book-labourers, college
employees, analysis-hands of whatever kind,
his book is a standing notice that the pre-
rogative of being immortal is granted by men,
even to a fool, if he has the grace not to know
it.   For that matter, even if the fool knows he
is a fool, if he cares more about his subject than
he cares about not letting any one else know it,
he is never forgotten.   The world cannot afford
to leave such a fool out.   Is it not a world in
which there is not a man living of us who does
not cherish in his heart a little secret like this of
his own? We are bound to admit that the main
difference between James Boswell and the rest,
consists in the fact that James Boswell found
something in the world so much more worth living for, than not letting the common secret out,
that he lived for it, and like all the other great
naives he will never get over living for it.

Even allowing that Boswell's consistent and unfailing motive in cultivating Samuel Johnson was vanity, this very vanity of Boswell's has more genius in it than Johnson's vocabulary, and the important and inspiring fact remains, that James Boswell, a flagrantly commonplace man in every single respect, by the law of letting himself go, has taken his stand forever in English literature, as the one commonplace man in it who has produced a work of genius. The main quality of a man of genius, his power of sacrificing everything to his main purpose, belonged to him. He was not only willing to seem the kind of fool he was, but he did not hesitate to seem several kinds that he was not, to fulfil his main purpose. That Samuel Johnson might be given the ponderous and gigantic and looming look that a Samuel Johnson ought to have, Boswell painted himself into his picture with more relentlessness than any other author that can be called to mind, except three or four similarly commonplace and similarly inspired and self-forgetful persons in the New Testament. There has never been any other biography in England with the single exception of Pepys, in which the author has so completely lost himself in his subject. If the author of Johnson's life had written his book with the inspiration of not being laughed at (which is the inspiration that nine out of ten who love to laugh are likely to write with), James Boswell would never have been heard of, and the burly figure of Samuel Johnson would be a blur behind a dictionary.

It may be set down as one of the necessary principles of the reading habit that no true and vital reading is possible except as the reader possesses and employs the gift of letting himself go. It is a gift that William Shakespeare and James Boswell and Elijah and Charles Lamb and a great many other happy but unimportant people have had in common. No man of genius—a man who puts his best and his most unconscious self into his utterance—can be read or listened to or interpreted for one moment without it. Except from those who bring to him the greeting of their own unconscious selves, he hides himself. He gives himself only to those with whom unconsciousness is a daily habit, with whom the joy of letting one's self go is one of the great resources of life. This joy is back of every great act and every deep appreciation in the world, and it is the charm and delight of the smaller ones. On its higher levels, it is called genius and inspiration. In religion it is called faith. It is the primal energy both of art and religion.

Probably only the man who has very little would be able to tell what faith is, as a basis of art or religion, but we have learned some things that it is not. We know that faith is not a dead-lift of the brain, a supreme effort either for God or for ourselves. It is the soul giving itself up, finding itself, feeling itself

drawn to its own, into infinite space, face to
face with strength. It is the supreme swing-
ing-free of the spirit, the becoming a part of
the running-gear of things. Faith is not an
act of the imagination—to the man who knows
it. It is infinite fact, the infinite crowding of
facts, the drawing of the man-self upward and
outward, where he is surrounded with the infinite man-self. Perhaps a man can make himself not believe. He can not make himself
believe. He can only believe by letting himself go, by trusting the force of gravity and
the law of space around him. Faith is the
universe flowing silently, implacably, through
his soul. He has given himself up to it. In
the tiniest, noisiest noon his spirit is flooded
with the stars. He is let out to the boundaries
of heaven and the night-sky bears him up in
the heat of the day.

In the presence of a great work of art—a
work of inspiration or faith, there is no such
thing as appreciation, without letting one's
self go.

II

The Subconscious Self

The criticism of Carlyle's remark, " Editors
are not here to say ' How,' "—that it is " ungracious and tantalisingly elusive," is a fair
illustration of the mood to which the habit of

analysis leads its victims. The explainer cannot let himself go. The puttering love of explaining and the need of explaining dog his
soul at every turn of thought or thought of
having a thought. He not only puts a microscope to his eyes to know with, but his eyes
have ingrown microscopes. The microscope
has become a part of his eyes. He cannot see
anything without putting it on a slide, and
when his microscope will not focus it, and it
cannot be reduced and explained, he explains
that it is not there.

The man of genius, on the other hand, with
whom truth is an experience instead of a specimen, has learned that the probabilities are that
the more impossible it is to explain a truth
the more truth there is in it. In so far as the
truth is an experience to him, he is not looking
for slides. He will not mount it as a specimen
and he is not interested in seeing it explained
or focussed. He lives with it in his own heart
in so far as he possesses it, and he looks at it
with a telescope for that greater part which he
cannot possess. The microscope is perpetually
mislaid. He has the experience itself and the
one thing he wants to do with it is to convey
it to others. He does this by giving himself
up to it. The truth having become a part of
him by his thus giving himself up, it becomes
a part of his reader, by his reader's giving
himself up.

Reading a work of genius is one man's unconsciousness greeting another man's. No author of the higher class can possibly be read without this mutual exchange of unconsciousness. He cannot be explained. He cannot explain himself. And he cannot be enjoyed, appreciated, or criticised by those who expect him to. Spiritual things are spiritually discerned, that is, experienced things are discerned by experience. They are " ungracious and tantalisingly elusive."

When the man who has a little talent tells a truth he tells the truth so ill that he is obliged to tell how to do it. The artist, on the other hand, having given himself up to the truth, almost always tells it as if he were listening to it, as if he were being borne up by it, as by some great delight, even while he speaks to us. It is the power of the artist's truth when he writes like this that it shall haunt his reader as it has haunted him. He lives with it and is haunted by it day after day whether he wants to be or not, and when a human being is obliged to live with a burning truth inside of him every day of his life, he will find a how for it, he will find some way of saying it, of getting it outside of him, of doing it, if only for the common and obvious reason that it burns the heart out of a man who does not. If the truth is really in a man—a truth to be done,—he finds out how to do it as a matter of self-preservation.

The average man no doubt will continue

now as always to consider Carlyle's " Editors
are not here to say ' How ' " ungracious and
tantalisingly elusive. He demands of every
writer not only that he shall write the truth
for every man but that he shall—practically—
read it for him—that is, tell him how to read
it—the best part of reading it. It is by this
explaining the truth too much, by making it
small enough for small people that so many lies
have been made out of it. The gist of the
matter seems to be that if the spirit of the truth
does not inspire a man to some more eager way
of finding out how to do a truth than asking
some other man how to do it, it must be some
other spirit. The way out for the explotterat-
ing or weak man does not consist in the scientist's or the commentator's how, or the
artist's how, or in any other strain of helping
the ground to hold one up. It consists in the
power of letting one's self go.

To say nothing of appreciation of power,
criticisim of power is impossible, without letting one's self go. Criticism which is not the
faithful remembering and reporting of an unconscious mood is not worthy of being called
criticism at all. A critic cannot find even the
faults of a book who does not let himself go in
it, and there is not a man living who can expect to write a criticism of a book until he has
given himself a chance to have an experience
with it, to write his criticism with. The larger
part of the professional criticism of the ages

that are past has proved worthless to us, because the typical professional critic has generally been a man who professes not to let
himself go and who is proud of it. If it were
not for the occasional possibility of his being
stunned by a book—made unconscious by it,—
the professional critic of the lesser sort would
never say anything of interest to us at all, and
even if he did, being a maimed and defective
conscious person, the evidence that he was
stunned is likely to be of more significance
than anything he may say about the book that
stunned him, or about the way he felt when he
was being stunned. Having had very little
practice in being unconscious, the bare fact is
all that he can remember about it. The unconsciousness of a person who has long lost the
habit of unconsciousness is apt to be a kind
of groping stupor or deadness at its best, and
not, as with the artist, a state of being, a way
of being incalculably alive, and of letting in
infinite life. It is a small joy that is not unconscious. The man who knows he is reading
when he has a book in his hands, does not
know very much about books.

People who always know what time it is, who
always know exactly where they are, and exactly how they look, have it not in their power
to read a great book. The book that comes to
the reader as a great book is always one that
shares with him the infinite and the eternal in
himself.

There is a time to know what time it is, and there is a time not to, and there are many places small enough to know where they are. The book that knows what time it is, in every sentence, will always be read by the clock, but the great book, the book with infinite vistas in it, shall not be read by men with a rim of time around it. The place of it is unmeasured, and there is no sound that men can make which shall tick in that place.

III

The Organic Principle of Inspiration

Letting one's self go is but a half-principle, however, to do one's reading with. The other half consists in getting one's self together again. In proportion as we truly appreciate what we read, we find ourselves playing at being Boswell to a book and being Johnson to it by turns. The vital reader lets himself go and collects himself as the work before him demands. There are some books, where it is necessary to let one's self go from beginning to end. There are others where a man may sit as he sits at a play, being himself between acts, or at proper intervals when the author lets down the curtain, and being translated the rest of the time.

Our richest moods are those in which, as we look back upon them, we seem to have been impressing, impressionable, creative, and receptive at the same time. The alternating currents of these moods are so swift that they seem simultaneous, and the immeasurable swiftness with which they pass from one to the other is the soul's instinctive method of kindling itself—the very act of inspiration. Sometimes the subconscious self has it all its own way with us except for a corner of dim, burning consciousness keeping guard. Sometimes the conscious has it all its own way with us and the subconscious self is crowded to the horizon's edge, like Northern Lights still playing in the distance; but the result is the same —the dim presence of one of these moods in the other, when one's power is least effective, and the gradual alternating of the currents of the moods as power grows more effective. In the higher states of power, the moods are seen alternating with increasing heat and swiftness until in the highest state of power of all, they are seen in their mutual glow and splendour, working as one mood, creating miracles.

The orator and the listener, the writer and the reader, in proportion as they become alive to one another, come into the same spirit—the spirit of mutual listening and utterance. At the very best, and in the most inspired mood, the reader reads as if he were a reader and

writer both, and the writer writes as if he were
a writer and reader both.

While it is necessary in the use and development of power, that all varieties and com-
binations of these moods should be familiar
experiences with the artist and with the reader
of the artist, it remains as the climax and
ideal of all energy and beauty in the human
soul that these moods shall be found alternating very swiftly — to all appearances together.
The artist's command of this alternating current, the swiftness with which he modulates
these moods into one another, is the measure
of his power. The violinist who plays best is
the one who sings the most things together in
his playing. He listens to his own bow, to
the heart of his audience, and to the soul of
the composer all at once. His instrument
sings a singing that blends them together.
The effect of their being together is called art.
The effect of their being together is produced
by the fact that they are together, that they
are born and living and dying together in the
man himself while the strings are singing to
us. They are the spirit within the strings.
His letting himself go to them, his gathering
himself out of them, his power to receive and
create at once, is the secret of the effect he
produces. The power to be receptive and
creative by turns is only obtained by constant
and daily practice, and when the modulating
of one of these moods into the other becomes a

swift and unconscious habit of life, what is called "temperament" in an artist is attained at last and inspiration is a daily occurrence. It is as hard for such a man to keep from being inspired as it is for the rest of us to make ourselves inspired. He has to go out of his way to avoid inspiration.

In proportion as this principle is recognised and allowed free play in the habits that obtain amongst men who know books, their habits will be inspired habits. Books will be read and lived in the same breath, and books that have been lived will be written.

The most serious menace in the present epidemic of analysis in our colleges is not that it is teaching men to analyse masterpieces until they are dead to them, but that it is teaching men to analyse their own lives until they are dead to themselves. When the process of education is such that it narrows the area of unconscious thinking and feeling in a man's life, it cuts him off from his kinship with the gods, from his habit of being unconscious enough of what he has to enter into the joy of what he has not.

The best that can be said of such an education is that it is a patient, painstaking, laborious training in locking one's self up. It dooms a man to himself, the smallest part of himself, and walls him out of the universe. He comes to its doorways one by one. The shining of them falls at first on him, as it falls on all of us. He sees the shining of them and hastens to them. One by one they are shut in his face. His soul is damned — is sentenced to perpetual consciousness of itself. What is there that he can do next? Turning round and round inside himself, learning how little worth while it is, there is but one fate left open to such a man, a blind and desperate lunge into the roar of the life he cannot see, for facts—the usual L.H.D., Ph.D. fate. If he piles around him the huge hollow sounding outsides of things in the universe that have lived, bones of soul, matter of bodies, skeletons of lives that men have lived, who shall blame him? He wonders why they have lived, why any one lives; and if, when he has wondered long enough why any one lives, we choose to make him the teacher of the young, that the young also may wonder why any one lives, why should we call him to account? He cannot but teach what he has, what has been given him, and we have but ourselves to thank that, as every radiant June comes round, diplomas for ennui are being handed out — thousands of them — to specially favoured children through all this broad and glorious land.

The Fourth Interference:
The Habit of Analysis

I

If Shakespeare Came to Chicago

IT is one of the supreme literary excellences of the Bible that, until the other day almost, it had never occurred to any one that it is literature at all. It has been read by men and women, and children and priests and popes, and kings and slaves and the dying of all ages, and it has come to them not as a book, but as if it were something happening to them.

It has come to them as nights and mornings come, and sleep and death, as one of the great, simple, infinite experiences of human life. It has been the habit of the world to take the greatest works of art, like the greatest works of God, in this simple and straight-forward fashion, as great experiences. If a masterpiece really is a masterpiece, and rains and shines its instincts on us as masterpieces should, we do not think whether it is literary or not, any more than we gaze on mountains and stop to think how sublimely scientific, raptly geological, and logically chemical they are. These things are true about mountains, and have their place. But it is the nature of a mountain to insist upon its own place—to be an experience first and to be as scientific and geological and chemical as it pleases afterward. It is the nature of anything powerful to be an experience first and to appeal to experience. When we have time, or when the experience is over, a mountain or a masterpiece can be analysed—the worst part of it; but we cannot make a masterpiece by analysing it; and a mountain has never been appreciated by pound-ing it into trap, quartz, and conglomerate; and it still holds good, as a general principle, that making a man appreciate a mountain by pound-ing it takes nearly as long as making the mountain, and is not nearly so worth while.

Not many years ago, in one of our journals of the more literary sort, there appeared a few directions from Chicago University to the late John Keats on how to write an " Ode to a Nightingale." These directions were from the Head of a Department, who, in a previous paper in the same journal, had rewritten the " Ode to a Grecian Urn." The main point the Head of the Department made, with regard to the nightingale, was that it was not worth rewriting. "'The Ode to the Nightingale,'" says he, "offers me no such temptation. There is almost nothing in it that properly belongs to the subject treated. The faults of the Grecian Urn are such as the poet himself, under wise criticism" (see catalogue of Chicago University) "might easily have removed. The faults of the Nightingale are such that they cannot be removed. They inhere in the idea and structure." The Head of the Department dwells at length upon "the hopeless fortune of the poem," expressing his regret that it can never be retrieved. After duly analysing what he considers the poem's leading thought, he regrets that a poet like John Keats should go so far, apropos of a nightingale, as to sigh in his immortal stanzas, "for something which, whatever it may be, is nothing short of a dead drunk."

One hears the soul of Keats from out its eternal Italy—

> "Is there no one near to help me?
>   . . . No fair dawn
> Of life from charitable voice? No sweet saying
> To set my dull and sadden'd spirit playing?"

The Head of the Department goes on, and the lines—

Still wouldst thou sing and I have ears in vain—
To thy high requiem become a sod—

are passed through analysis. "What the fit-
ness is," he says, "or what the poetic or other
effectiveness of suggesting that the corpse of a
person who has ceased upon the midnight still
has ears, only to add that it has them in vain, I
cannot pretend to understand"—one of a great
many other things that the Head of the Department does not pretend to understand. It
is probably with the same outfit of not pretend-
ing to understand that—for the edification of
the merely admiring mind — the "Ode to a
Grecian Urn" was rewritten. To Keats's
lines—

Oh, Attic shape! Fair attitude! with brede
Of marble men and maidens overwrought,
With forest branches and the trodden weed;
Thou, silent form, dost tease us out of thought
As doth eternity: Cold Pastoral!
When old age shall this generation waste,
Thou shalt remain, in midst of other woe
Than ours, a friend to man, to whom thou sayest,
"Beauty is truth, truth beauty"—that is all
Ye know on earth, and all ye need to know—

he makes various corrections, offering as a
substitute-conclusion to the poet's song the
following outburst:

Preaching this wisdom with thy cheerful mien:
Possessing beauty thou possessest all;
Pause at that goal, nor farther push thy quest.

It would not be just to the present state of academic instruction in literature to illustrate it by such an extreme instance as this of the damage the educated mind—debauched with analysis—is capable of doing to the reading habit. It is probable that a large proportion of the teachers of literature in the United States, both out of their sense of John Keats and out of respect to themselves, would have publicly resented this astonishing exhibit of the extreme literary-academic mind in a prominent journal, had they not suspected that its editor, having discovered a literary-academic mind that could take itself as seriously as this, had deliberately brought it out as a spectacle. It could do no harm to Keats, certainly, or to any one else, and would afford an infinite deal of amusement—the journal argued—to let a mind like this clatter down a column to oblivion. So it did. It was taken by all concerned, teachers, critics, and observers alike, as one of the more interesting literary events of the season.

Unfortunately, however, entertainments of this kind have a very serious side to them. It is one thing to smile at an individual when one knows that standing where he does he stands by himself, and another to smile at an individual when one knows that he is not standing by himself, that he is a type, that there must be a great many others like him or he would not be standing where he does at all. When a human being is seen taking his stand over his own soul in public print, summing up its emptiness there, and gloating over it, we are in the presence of a disheartening fact. It can be covered up, however, and in what, on the whole, is such a fine, true-ringing, hearty old world as this, it need not be made much of; but when we find that a mind like this has been placed at the head of a Department of Poetry in a great, representative American university, the last thing that should be done with it is to cover it up. The more people know where the analytical mind is to-day—where it is getting to be—and the more they think what its being there means, the better. The signs of the timés, the destiny of education, and the fate of literature are all involved in a fact like this. The mere possibility of having the analysing-grinding mind engaged in teaching a spontaneous art in a great educational institution would be of great significance. The fact that it is actually there and that no particular comment is excited by its being there, is significant. It betrays not only what the general, national, academic attitude toward literature is, but that that attitude has become habitual, that it is taken for granted.

One would be inclined to suppose, looking at the matter abstractly, that all students and teachers of literature would take it for granted that the practice of making a dispassionate criticism of a passion would be a dangerous practice for any vital and spontaneous nature —certainly the last kind of practice that a student of the art of poetry (that is, the art of literature, in the essential sense) would wish to make himself master of. The first item in a critic's outfit for criticising a passion is having one. The fact that this is not regarded as an axiom in our current education in books is a very significant fact. It goes with another significant fact — the assumption, in most courses of literature as at present conducted, that a little man (that is, a man incapable of a great passion), who is not even able to read a book with a great passion in it, can somehow teach other people to read it.

It is not necessary to deny that analysis occasionally plays a valuable part in bringing a pupil to a true method and knowledge of literature, but unless the analysis is inspired nothing can be more dangerous to a pupil under his thirtieth year, even for the shortest period of time, or more likely to move him over to the farthest confines of the creative life, or more certain, if continued long enough, to set him forever outside all power or possibility of power, either in the art of literature or in any of the other arts.

The first objection to the analysis of one of Shakespeare's plays as ordinarily practised in courses of literature is that it is of doubtful value to nine hundred and ninety-nine pupils in a thousand—if they do it. The second is, that they cannot do it. The analysing of one of Shakespeare's plays requires more of a commonplace pupil than Shakespeare required of himself. The apology that is given for the analysing method is, that the process of analysing a work of Shakespeare's will show the pupil how Shakespeare did it, and that by seeing how Shakespeare did it he will see how to do it himself.

In the first place, analysis will not show how Shakespeare did it, and in the second place, if it does, it will show that he did not do it by analysis. In the third place,—to say nothing of not doing it by analysis,—if he had analysed it before he did it, he could not have analysed it afterward in the literal and modern sense. In the fourth place, even if Shakespeare were able to do his work by analysing it before he did it, it does not follow that undergraduate students can.

A man of genius, with all his onset of natural passion, his natural power of letting himself go, could doubtless do more analysing, both before and after his work, than any one else without being damaged by it. What shall be said of the folly of trying to teach men of talent, and the mere pupils of men of talent, by analysis—by a method, that is, which, even if it succeeds in doing what it tries to do, can only, at the very best, reveal to the pupil the roots of his instincts before they have come up? And why is it that our courses of literature may be seen assuming to-day on every hand, almost without exception, that by teaching men to analyse their own inspirations—the inspirations they have—and teaching them to analyse the inspirations of other men—inspirations they can never have—we are somehow teaching them "English literature"?

It seems to have been overlooked while we are all analytically falling at Shakespeare's feet, that Shakespeare did not become Shakespeare by analytically falling at any one's feet —not even at his own—and that the most important difference between being a Shakespeare and being an analyser of Shakespeare is that with the man Shakespeare no submitting of himself to the analysis-gymnast would ever have been possible, and with the students of Shakespeare (as students go and if they are caught young enough) the habit of analysis is not only a possibility but a sleek, industrious, and complacent certainty.

After a little furtive looking backward perhaps, and a few tremblings and doubts, they shall all be seen, almost to a man, offering their souls to Moloch, as though the not having a soul and not missing it were the one final and consummate triumph that literary culture could bring. Flocks of them can be seen with the shining in their faces year after year, term after term, almost anywhere on the civilised globe, doing this very thing—doing it under the impression that they are learning something, and not until the shining in their faces is gone will they be under the impression that they have learned it (whatever it is) and that they are educated.

The fact that the analytic mind is establishing itself, in a greater or less degree, as the sentinel in college life of the entire creative literature of the world is a fact with many meanings in it. It means not only that there are a great many more minds like it in literature, but that a great many other minds—nearly all college-educated minds—are being made like it. It means that unless the danger is promptly faced and acted upon the next generation of American citizens can neither expect to be able to produce literature of its own nor to appreciate or enjoy literature that has been produced. It means that another eighteenth century is coming to the world; and, as the analysis is deeper than before and more deadly-clever with the deeper things than before, it is going to be the longest eighteenth century the world has ever seen—generations with machines for hands and feet, machines for minds, machines outside their minds to enjoy the machines inside their minds with. Every man with his information-machine to be cultured with, his religious machine to be good with, and his private Analysis Machine to be beautiful with, shall take his place in the world—shall add his soul to the Machine we make a world with. For every man that is born on the earth one more joy shall be crowded out of it—one more analysis of joy shall take its place, go round and round under the stars —dew, dawn, and darkness—until it stops. How a sunrise is made and why a cloud is artistic and how pines should be composed in a landscape, all men shall know. We shall criticise the technique of thunderstorms. "And what is a sunset after all?" The reflection of a large body on rarefied air. Through analysed heaven and over analysed fields it trails its joylessness around the earth.

Time was, when the setting of the sun was the playing of two worlds upon a human being's life on the edge of the little day, the blending of sense and spirit for him, earth and heaven, out in the still west. His whole being went forth to it. He watched with it and prayed and sang with it. In its presence his soul walked down to the stars. Out of the joy of his life, the finite sorrow and the struggle of his life, he gazed upon it. It was the portrait of his infinite self. Every setting sun that came to him was a compact with Eternal Joy. The Night itself—his figure faint before it in the flicker of the east — whispered to him: "Thou also—hills and heavens around thee, hills and heavens within thee—oh, Child of Time—Thou also art God!"

"Ah me! How I could love! My soul doth melt," cries Keats:

Ye deaf and senseless minutes of the day,
And thou old forest, hold ye this for true,

There is no lightning, no authentic dew
But in the eye of love; there 's not a sound,
Melodious howsoever, can confound
The heavens and the earth to such a death
As doth the voice of love; there 's not a breath
Will mingle kindly with the meadow air,
Till it has panted round, and stolen a share
Of passion from the heart.

John Keats and William Shakespeare wrote masterpieces because they had passions, spiritual experiences, and the daily habit of inspiration. In so far as these masterpieces are being truthfully taught, they are taught by teachers who themselves know the passion of creation. They teach John Keats and William Shakespeare by rousing the same passions and experiences in the pupil that Keats and Shakespeare had, and by daily appealing to them.

II

Analysis Analysed

There are a great many men in the world to-day, faithfully doing their stint in it (they are commonly known as men of talent), who would have been men of genius if they had dared. Education has made cowards of us all, and the habit of examining the roots of one's instincts, before they come up, is an incurable habit.

The essential principle in a true work of art is always the poem or the song that is hidden in it. A work of art by a man of talent is generally ranked by the fact that it is the work of a man who analyses a song before he sings it. He puts down the words of the song first—writes it, that is—in prose. Then he lumbers it over into poetry. Then he looks around for some music for it. Then he practises at singing it, and then he sings it. The man of genius, on the other hand, whether he be a great one or a very little one, is known by the fact that he has a song sent to him. He sings it. He has a habit of humming it over afterwards. His humming it over afterwards is his analysis. It is the only possible inspired analysis.

The difference between these two types of men is so great that anything that the smaller of them has to say about the spirit or the processes of the other is of little value. When one of them tries to teach the work of the other, which is what almost always occurs,—the man of talent being the typical professor of works of genius,—the result is fatal. A singer who is so little capable of singing that he can give a prose analysis of his own song while it is coming to him and before he sings it, can hardly be expected to extemporise an inspired analysis of another man's song after reading it. If a man cannot apply inspired analysis to a little common passion in a song he has of his own, he is placed in a hopeless position when he tries to give an inspired

analysis of a passion that only another man
could have and that only a great man would
forget himself long enough to have.

An inspired analysis may be defined as the
kind of analysis that the real poet in his crea-
tively critical mood is able to give to his work
—a low-singing or humming analysis in which
all the elements of the song are active and all
the faculties and all the senses work on the
subject at once. The proportions and relations
of a living thing are all kept perfect in an inspired analysis, and the song is made perfect
at last, not by being taken apart, but by being
made to pass its delight more deeply and more
slowly through the singer's utmost self to its
fulfilment.

What is ordinarily taught as analysis is very
different from this. It consists in the deliber-
ate and triumphant separation of the faculties
from one another and from the thing they have
produced—the dull, bare, pitiless process of
passing a living and beautiful thing before one
vacant, staring faculty at a time. This faculty,
being left in the stupor of being all by itself,
sits in complacent judgment upon a work of
art, the very essence of the life and beauty of
which is its appealing to all of the faculties
and senses at once, in their true proportion,
glowing them together into a unit—namely,
several things made into one thing, that is—
several things occupying the same time and
the same place, that is—synthesis. An in-

spired analysis is the rehearsal of a synthesis. An analysis is not inspired unless it comes as a flash of light and a burst of music and a breath of fragrance all in one. Such an analysis cannot be secured with painstaking and slowness, unless the painstaking and slowness are the rehearsal of a synthesis, and all the elements in it are laboured on and delighted in at once. It must be a low-singing or humming analysis.

The expert student or teacher of poetry who makes "a dispassionate criticism" of a passion, who makes it his special boast that he is able to apply his intellect severely by itself to a great poem, boasts of the devastation of the highest power a human being can attain. The commonest man that lives, whatever his powers may be, if they are powers that act together, can look down on a man whose powers cannot, as a mutilated being. While it cannot be denied that a being who has been thus especially mutilated is often possessed of a certain literary ability, he belongs to the acrobats of literature rather than to literature itself. The contortionist who separates himself from his hands and feet for the delectation of audiences, the circus performer who makes a battering-ram of his head and who glories in being shot out of a cannon into space and amazement, goes through his motions with essentially the same pride in his strength, and sustains the same relation to the strength of the real man of the world.

Whatever a course of literary criticism may be, or its value may be, to the pupils who take it, it consists, more often than not, on the part of pupil and teacher both, in the dislocating of one faculty from all the others, and the bearing it down hard on a work of art, as if what it was made of, or how it was made, could only be seen by scratching it.

It is to be expected now and then, in the hurry of the outside world, that a newspaper critic will be found writing a cerebellum criticism of a work of the imagination; but the student of literature, in the comparative quiet and leisure of the college atmosphere, who works in the same separated spirit, who estimates a work by dislocating his faculties on it, is infinitely more blameworthy; and the college teacher who teaches a work of genius by causing it to file before one of his faculties at a time, when all of them would not be enough,—who does this in the presence of young persons and trains them to do it themselves,—is a public menace. The attempt to master a masterpiece, as it were, by reading it first with the sense of sight, and then with the sense of smell, and with all the senses in turn, keeping them carefully guarded from their habit of sensing things together, is not only a self-destructive but a hopeless attempt. A great mind, even if it would attempt to master anything in this way, would find it hopeless, and the attempt to learn a great work of art—a great whole—by

Analysis
Analysed

applying the small parts of a small mind to it, one after the other, is more hopeless still. It can be put down as a general principle that a human being who is so little alive that he finds his main pleasure in life in taking himself apart, can find little of value for others in a masterpiece—a work of art which is so much alive that it cannot be taken apart, and which is eternal because its secret is eternally its own. If the time ever comes when it can be taken apart, it will be done only by a man who could have put it together, who is more alive than the masterpiece is alive. Until the masterpiece meets with a master who is more creative than its first master was, the less the motions of analysis are gone through with by those who are not masters, the better. A masterpiece cannot be analysed by the cold and negative process of being taken apart. It can only be analysed by being melted down. It can only be melted down by a man who has creative heat in him to melt it down and the daily habit of glowing with creative heat.

It is a matter of common observation that the fewer resources an artist has, the more things there are in nature and in the nature of life which he thinks are not beautiful. The making of an artist is his sense of selection. If he is an artist of the smaller type, he selects beautiful subjects—subjects with ready-made beauty in them. If he is an artist of the larger type, he can hardly miss making almost any

subject beautiful, because he has so many
beautiful things to put it with.   He sees every
subject the way it is—that is, in relation to a
great many other subjects—the way God saw
it, when He made it, and the way it is.

The essential difference between a small
mood and a large one is that in the small one
we see each thing we look on, comparatively
by itself, or with reference to one or two relations to persons and events.   In our larger
mood we see it less analytically.   We see it as
it is and as it lives and as a god would see it,
playing its meaning through the whole created
scheme into everything else.

The soul of beauty is synthesis.   In the
presence of a mountain the sound of a hammer
is as rich as a symphony.   It is like the little
word of a great man, great in its great relations.
When the spirit is waked and the man within
the man is listening to it, the sound of a hoof
on a lonely road in the great woods is the
footstep of cities to him coming through the
trees, and the low, chocking sound of a cart-
wheel in the still and radiant valley throngs
his being like an opera.   All sights and echoes
and thoughts and feelings revel in it.   It is
music for the smoke, rapt and beautiful, rising
from the chimneys at his feet.   A sheet of water
—making heaven out of nothing — is beautiful
to the dullest man, because he cannot analyse it,
could not—even if he would—contrive to see it
by itself.   Skies come crowding on it.   There

is enough poetry in the mere angle of a sinking sun to flood the prose of a continent with, because the gentle earthlong shadows that follow it lay their fingers upon all life and creep together innumerable separated things.

In the meadow where our birds are there is scarcely a tree in sight to tangle the singing in. It is a meadow with miles of sunlight in it. It seems like a kind of world-melody to walk in the height of noon there — infinite grass, infinite sky, gusts of bobolinks' voices—it's as if the air that drifted down made music of itself; and the song of all the singing everywhere—the song the soul hears—comes on the slow winds.

Half the delight of a bobolink is that he is more synthetic, more of a poet, than other birds,—has a duet in his throat. He bursts from the grass and sings in bursts—plays his own obligato while he goes. One can never see him in his eager flurry, between his low heaven and his low nest, without catching the lilt of inspiration. Like the true poet, he suits the action to the word in a weary world, and does his flying and singing together. The song that he throws around him, is the very spirit of his wings—of all wings. More beauty is always the putting of more things together. They were created to be together. The spirit of art is the spirit that finds this out. Even the bobolink is cosmic, if he sings with room enough; and when the heart wakes the song of the cricket is infinite. We hear it across stars.

The Fifth Interference : Literary Drill in College

I

Seeds and Blossoms

FOUR men stood before God at the end of The First Week, watching Him whirl His little globe.* The first man said to Him, "Tell me how you did it." The second man said, "Let me have it." The third man said, "What is it for?" The fourth man said nothing, and fell down and worshipped. Having worshipped he rose to his feet and made a world himself.

These four men have been known in history as the Scientist, the Man of Affairs, the Philosopher, and the Artist. They stand for the four necessary points of view in reading books.

---

* Recently discovered manuscript.

Most of the readers of the world are content to be partitioned off, and having been duly set down for life in one or the other of these four divisions of human nature they take sides from beginning to end with one or the other of these four men. It is the distinction of the scholar of the highest class in every period, that he declines to do this. In so far as he finds each of the four men taking sides against each other, he takes sides against each of them in behalf of all. He insists on being able to absorb knowledge, to read and write in all four ways. If he is a man of genius as well as a scholar, he insists on being able to read and write, as a rule, in all four ways at once; if his genius is of the lesser kind, in two or three ways at once. The eternal books are those that stand this four-sided test. They are written from all of these points of view. They have absorbed into themselves the four moods of creation morning. It is thus that they bring the morning back to us.

The most important question in regard to books that our schools and institutions of learning are obliged to face at present is, "How shall we produce conditions that will enable the ordinary man to keep the proportions that belong to a man, to absorb knowledge, to do his reading and writing in all four ways at once?" In other words, How shall we enable him to be a natural man, a man of genius as far as he goes?

A masterpiece is a book that can only be read by a man who is a master in some degree of the things the book is master of. The man who has mastered things the most is the man who can make those things. The man who makes things is the artist. He has bowed down and worshipped and he has arisen and stood before God and created before Him, and the spirit of the Creator is in him. To take the artist's point of view, is to take the point of view that absorbs and sums up the others. The supremacy and comprehensiveness of this point of view is a matter of fact rather than argument. The artist is the man who makes the things that Science and Practical Affairs and Philosophy are merely about. The artist of the higher order is more scientific than the scientist, more practical than the man of affairs, and more philosophic than the philosopher, because he combines what these men do about things, and what these men say about things, into the things themselves, and makes the things live.

To combine these four moods at once in one's attitude toward an idea is to take the artist's—that is, the creative—point of view toward it. The only fundamental outfit a man can have for reading books in all four ways at once is his ability to take the point of view of the man who made the book in all four ways at once, and feel the way he felt when he made it.

The organs that appreciate literature are the organs that made it. True reading is latent writing. The more one feels like writing a book when he reads it the more alive his reading is and the more alive the book is.

The measure of culture is its originating and reproductive capacity, the amount of seed and blossom there is in it, the amount it can afford to throw away, and secure divine results. Unless the culture in books we are taking such national pains to acquire in the present generation can be said to have this pollen quality in it, unless it is contagious, can be summed up in its pollen and transmitted, unless it is nothing more or less than life itself made catching, unless, like all else that is allowed to have rights in nature, it has powers also, has an almost infinite power of self-multiplication, self-perpetuation, the more cultured we are the more emasculated we are. The vegetables of the earth and the flowers of the field—the very codfish of the sea become our superiors. What is more to the point, in the minds and interests of all living human beings, their culture crowds ours out.

Nature may be somewhat coarse and simple-minded and naïve, but reproduction is her main point and she never misses it. Her prejudice against dead things is immutable. If a man objects to this prejudice against dead things, his only way of making himself count is to die. Nature uses such men over again, makes them into something more worth while, something terribly or beautifully alive,—and goes on her way.

If this principle—namely, that the reproductive power of culture is the measure of its value—were as fully introduced and recognised in the world of books as it is in the world of commerce and in the natural world, it would revolutionise from top to bottom, and from entrance examination to diploma, the entire course of study, policy, and spirit of most of our educational institutions. Allowing for exceptions in every faculty—memorable to all of us who have been college students,—it would require a new corps of teachers.

Entrance examinations for pupils and teachers alike would determine two points. First, what does this person know about things? Second, what is the condition of his organs—what can he do with them? If the privilege of being a pupil in the standard college were conditioned strictly upon the second of these questions—the condition of his organs —as well as upon the first, fifty out of a hundred pupils, as prepared at present, would fall short of admission. If the same test were applied for admission to the faculty, ninety out of a hundred teachers would fall short of admission. Having had analytic, self-destructive, learned habits for a longer time than their pupils, the condition of their organs is more hopeless.

The man who has the greatest joy in a symphony is:

First, the man who composes it.

Second, the conductor.

Third, the performers.

Fourth, those who might be composers of such music themselves.

Fifth, those in the audience who have been performers.

Sixth, those who are going to be.

Seventh, those who are composers of such music for other instruments.

Eighth, those who are composers of music in other arts—literature, painting, sculpture, and architecture.

Ninth, those who are performers of music on other instruments.

Tenth, those who are performers of music in other arts.

Eleventh, those who are creators of music with their own lives.

Twelfth, those who perform and interpret in their own lives the music they hear in other lives.

Thirteenth, those who create anything whatever and who love perfection in it.

Fourteenth, " The Public."

Fifteenth, the Professional Critic — almost inevitably at the fifteenth remove from the heart of things because he is the least creative, unless he is a man of genius, or has pluck and talent enough to work his way through the

other fourteen moods and sum them up before
he ventures to criticise.

The principles that have been employed in
putting life into literature must be employed
on drawing life out of it.   These principles are
the creative principles—principles of joy.   All
influences in education, family training, and a
man's life that tend to overawe, crowd out,
and make impossible his own private, personal,
daily habit of creative joy are the enemies of
books.

II

Private Road: Dangerous

The impotence of the study of literature as
practised in the schools and colleges of the
present day turns largely on the fact that the
principle of creative joy—of knowing through
creative joy—is overlooked.   The field of vision
is the book and not the world.   In the average
course in literature the field is not even the
book.   It is still farther from the creative
point of view.   It is the book about the book.

It is written generally in the laborious, un-
readable, well-read style—the book about the
book.   You are as one (when you are in the
book about the book) thrust into the shadow
of the endless aisles of Other Books—not that
they are referred to baldly, or vulgarly, or in
the text.   It is worse than this (for this could

be skipped). But you are surrounded help-lessly. Invisible lexicons are on every page. Grammars and rhetorics, piled up in para-graphs and between the lines thrust at you everywhere. Hardly a chapter that does not convey its sense of struggling faithfulness, of infinite forlorn and empty plodding—and all for something a man might have known any-way. "I have toted a thousand books," each chapter seems to say. "This one paragraph [page 1993 — you feel it in the paragraph] has had to have forty-seven books carried to it." Not once, except in loopholes in his read-ing which come now and then, does the face of the man's soul peep forth. One does not ex-pect to meet any one in the book about the book—not one's self, not even the man who writes it, nor the man who writes the book that the book is about. One is confronted with a mob.

Two things are apt to be true of students who study the great masters in courses em-ploying the book about the book. Even if the books about the book are what they ought to be, the pupils of such courses find that (1) studying the master, instead of the things he mastered, they lose all power over the things he mastered; (2) they lose, consequently, not only the power of creating masterpieces out of these things themselves, but the power of enjoying those that have been created by others, of having the daily experiences that make such joy possible. They are out of range of experience. They are barricaded against life. Inasmuch as the creators of literature, without a single exception, have been more interested in life than in books, and have written books to help other people to be more interested in life than in books, this is the gravest possible defect. To be more interested in life than in books is the first essential for creating a book or for understanding one.

The typical course of study now offered in literature carries on its process of paralysis in various ways:

First. It undermines the imagination by giving it paper things instead of real ones to work on.

Second. By seeing that these things are selected instead of letting the imagination select its own things — the essence of having an imagination.

Third. By requiring of the student a rigorous and ceaselessly unimaginative habit. The paralysis of the learned is forced upon him. He finds little escape from the constant reading of books that have all the imagination left out of them.

Fourth. By forcing the imagination to work so hard in its capacity of pack-horse and memory that it has no power left to go anywhere of itself.

Fifth. By overawing individual initiative, undermining personality in the pupil, crowding great classics into him instead of attracting little ones out of him. Attracting little classics out of a man is a thing that great classics are always intended to do—the thing that they always succeed in doing when left to themselves.

Sixth. The teacher of literature so-called, having succeeded in destroying the personality of the pupil, puts himself in front of the personality of the author.

Seventh. A teacher who destroys personality in a pupil is the wrong personality to put in front of an author. If he were the right one, if he had the spirit of the author, his being in front, now and then at least, would be interpretation and inspiration. Not having the spirit of the author, he is intimidated by him, or has all he can do not to be. A classic cannot reveal itself to a groveller or to a critic. It is a book that was written standing up and it can only be studied and taught by those who stand up without knowing it. The decorons and beautiful despising of one's self that the study of the classics has come to be as conducted under unclassic teachers, is a fact that speaks for itself.

Eighth. Even if the personality of the teacher of literature is so fortunate as not to be the wrong one, there is not enough of it. There is hardly a course of literature that can be found in a college catalogue at the present time that does not base itself on the dictum that a great book can somehow — by some

Private
Road :
Dangerous

mysterious process—be taught by a small person. The axiom that necessarily undermines all such courses is obvious enough. A great book cannot be taught except by a teacher who is literally living in a great spirit, the spirit the great book lived in before it became a book,—a teacher who has the great book in him—not over him,—who, if he took time for it, might be capable of writing, in some sense at least, a great book himself. When the teacher is a teacher of this kind, teaches the spirit of what he teaches — that is, teaches the inside,— a classic can be taught.

Otherwise the best course in literature that can be devised is the one that gives the masterpieces the most opportunity to teach themselves. The object of a course in literature is best served in proportion as the course is arranged and all associated studies are arranged in such a way as to secure sensitive and contagious conditions for the pupil's mind in the presence of the great masters, such conditions as give the pupil time, freedom, space, and atmosphere—the things out of which a masterpiece is written and with which alone it can be taught, or can teach itself.

All that comes between a masterpiece and its thus teaching itself, spreads ruin both ways. The masterpiece is partitioned off from the pupil, guarded to be kept aloof from him —outside of him. The pupil is locked up from himself—his possible self.

Not too much stress could possibly be laid upon intimacy with the great books or on the constant habit of living on them. They are the movable Olympus. All who create camp out between the heavens and the earth on them and breathe and live and climb upon them. From their mighty sides they look down on human life. But classics can only be taught by classics. The creative paralysis of pupils who have drudged most deeply in classical training—English or otherwise—is a fact that no observer of college life can overlook. The guilt for this state of affairs must be laid at the door of the classics or at the door of the teachers. Either the classics are not worth teaching or they are not being taught properly.

In either case the best way out of the difficulty would seem to be for teachers to let the classics teach themselves, to furnish the students with the atmosphere, the conditions, the points of view in life, which will give the classics a chance to teach themselves.

This brings us to the important fact that teachers of literature do not wish to create the atmosphere, the conditions, and points of view that give the classics a chance to teach themselves. Creating the atmosphere for a classic in the life of a student is harder than creating a classic. The more obvious and practicable course is to teach the classic—teach it one's self, whether there is atmosphere or not.

It is admitted that this is not the ideal way

to do with college students who suppose they are studying literature, but it is contended— college students and college electives being what they are—that there is nothing else to do. The situation sums itself up in the atti- tude of self-defence. "It may be (as no one needs to point out), that the teaching of litera- ture, as at present conducted in college, is a somewhat faithful and dogged farce, but what- ever may be the faults of modern college- teaching in literature, it is as good as our pupils deserve." In other words, the teachers are not respecting their pupils. It may be said to be the constitution and by-laws of the litera- ture class (as generally conducted) that the teachers cannot and must not respect their pupils. They cannot afford to. It costs more than most pupils are mentally worth, it is plausibly contended, to furnish students in college with the conditions of life and the con- ditions in their own minds that will give mas- terpieces a fair chance at them. *Ergo*, inas- much as the average pupil cannot be taught a classic he must be choked with it.

The fact that the typical teacher of literature is more or less grudgingly engaged in doing his work and conducting his classes under the practical working theory that his pupils are not good enough for him, suggests two import- ant principles.

First. If his pupils are good enough for him, they are good enough to be taught the best there is in him, and they must be taught this best there is in him, as far as it goes, whether all of them are good enough for it or not. There is as much learning in watching others being educated as there is in appearing to be educated one's self.

Second. If his pupils are not good enough for him, the most literary thing he can do with them is to make them good enough. If he is not a sufficiently literary teacher to divine the central ganglion of interest in a pupil, and play upon it and gather delight about it and make it gather delight itself, the next most literary thing he can do is protect both the books and the pupil by keeping them faithfully apart until they are ready for one another.

If the teacher cannot recognise, arouse, and exercise such organs as his pupil has, and carry them out into themselves, and free them in self-activity, the pupil may be unfortunate in not having a better teacher, but he is fortunate in having no better organs to be blundered on.

The drawing out of a pupil's first faint but honest and lasting power of really reading a book, of knowing what it is to be sensitive to a book, does not produce a very literary-looking result, of course, and it is hard to give the result an impressive or learned look in a catalogue, and it is a difficult thing to do without considering each pupil as a special human being by himself,—worthy of some attention on that account,—but it is the one upright, worthy,

and beautiful thing a teacher can do.   Any
easier course he may choose to adopt in an institution of learning (even when it is taken help-
lessly or thoughtlessly as it generally is) is insin-
cere and spectacular, a despising not only of the
pupil but of the college public and of one's self.

If it is true that the right study of literature
consists in exercising and opening out the human mind instead of making it a place for cold
storage, it is not necessary to call attention to
the essential pretentiousness and shoddiness of
the average college course in literature.   At
its best—that is, if the pupils do not do the
work, the study of literature in college is a
sorry spectacle enough—a kind of huge girls'
school with a chaperone taking its park walk.
At its worst—that is, when the pupils do do
the work, it is a sight that would break a
Homer's heart.   If it were not for a few inspired and inconsistent teachers blessing particular schools and scholars here and there,
doing a little guilty, furtive teaching, whether
or no, discovering short-cuts, climbing fences,
breaking through the fields, and walking on
the grass, the whole modern scheme of elaborate, tireless, endless laboriousness would come
to nothing, except the sight of larger piles of
paper in the world, perhaps, and rows of dreary,
dogged people with degrees lugging them back
and forth in it,—one pile of paper to another
pile of paper, and a general sense that something is being done.

In the meantime, human life around us, trudging along in its anger, sorrow, or bliss, wonders what this thing is that is being done, and has a vague and troubled respect for it; but it is to be noted that it buys and reads the books (and that it has always bought and read the books) of those who have not done it, and who are not doing it,—those who, standing in the spectacle of the universe, have been sensitive to it, have had a mighty love in it, or a mighty hate, or a true experience, and who have laughed and cried with it through the hearts of their brothers to the ends of the earth.

III

The Organs of Literature

The literary problem—the problem of possessing or appreciating or teaching a literary style—resolves itself at last into a pure problem of personality. A pupil is being trained in literature in proportion as his spiritual and physical powers are being brought out by the teacher and played upon until they permeate each other in all that he does and in all that he is—in all phases of his life. Unless what a pupil is glows to the finger tips of his words, he cannot write, and unless what he is makes the words of other men glow when he reads, he cannot read.

In proportion as it is great, literature is addressed to all of a man's body and to all of his soul. It matters nothing how much a man may know about books, unless the pages of them play upon his senses while he reads, he is not physically a cultivated man, a gentleman, or scholar with his body. Unless books play upon all his spiritual and mental sensibilities when he reads he cannot be considered a cultivated man, a gentleman, and a scholar in his soul. It is the essence of all great literature that it makes its direct appeal to sense-perceptions permeated with spiritual suggestion. There is no such thing possible as being a literary authority, a cultured or scholarly man, unless the permeating of the sense-perceptions with spiritual suggestion is a daily and unconscious habit of life. "Every man his own poet" is the underlying assumption of every genuine work of art, and a work of art cannot be taught to a pupil in any other way than by making this same pupil a poet, by getting him to discover himself. Continued and unfaltering disaster is all that can be expected of all methods of literary training that do not recognise this.

To teach a pupil all that can be known about a great poem is to take the poetry out of him, and to make the poem prose to him forever. A pupil cannot even be taught great prose except by making a poet of him, in his attitude toward it, and by so governing the conditions, excitements, duties, and habits of his course of study that he will discover he is a poet in spite of himself. The essence of Walter Pater's essays cannot be taught to a pupil except by making a new creature of him in the presence of the things the essays are about. Unless the conditions of a pupil's course are so governed, in college or otherwise, as to insure and develop the delicate and strong response of all his bodily senses, at the time of his life when nature decrees that his senses must be developed, that the spirit must be waked in them, or not at all, the study of Walter Pater will be in vain.

The physical organisation, the mere bodily state of the pupil, necessary to appreciate either the form or the substance of a bit of writing like *The Child in the House*, is the first thing a true teacher is concerned with. A college graduate whose nostrils have not been trained for years,—steeped in the great, still delights of the ground,—who has not learned the spirit and fragrance of the soil beneath his feet, is not a sufficiently cultivated person to pronounce judgment either upon Walter Pater's style or upon his definition of style.

To be educated in the great literatures of the world is to be trained in the drawing out in one's own body and mind of the physical and mental powers of those who write great literatures. Culture is the feeling of the in-duced current—the thrill of the lives of the dead—the charging the nerves of the body and powers of the spirit with the genius that has walked the earth before us. In the borrowed glories of the great for one swift and passing page we walk before heaven with them, breathe the long breath of the centuries with them, know the joy of the gods and live. The man of genius is the man who literally gives himself. He makes every man a man of genius for the time being. He exchanges souls with us and for one brief moment we are great, we are beautiful, we are immortal. We are visited with our possible selves. Literature is the transfiguring of the senses in which men are dwelling every day and of the thoughts of the mind in which they are living every day. It is the commingling of one's life in one vast network of sensibility, communion, and eternal comradeship with all the joy and sorrow, taste, odor, and sound, passion of men and love of women and worship of God, that ever has been on the earth, since the watching of the first night above the earth, or since the look of the first morning on it, when it was loved for the first time by a human life.

The artist is recognised as an artist in proportion as the senses of his body drift their glow and splendour over into the creations of his mind. He is an artist because his flesh is informed with the spirit, because in whatever he does he incarnates the spirit in the flesh.

The gentle, stroking delight in this universe

that Dr. Holmes took all his days, his contagious gladness in it and approval of it, his impressionableness to its moods—its Oliver-Wendell ones,—who really denies in his soul that this capacity of Dr. Holmes to enjoy, this delicate, ceaseless tasting with sense and spirit of the essence of life, was the very substance of his culture? The books that he wrote and the things that he knew were merely the form of it. His power of expression was the blending of sense and spirit in him, and because his mind was trained into the texture of his body people delighted in his words in form and spirit both.

There is no training in the art of expression or study of those who know how to express, that shall not consist, not in a pupil's knowing wherein the power of a book lies, but in his experiencing the power himself, in his entering the life behind the book and the habit of life that made writing such a book and reading it possible. This habit is the habit of incarnation.

A true and classic book is always the history some human soul has had in its tent of flesh, camped out beneath the stars, groping for the thing they shine to us, trying to find a body for it. In the great wide plain of wonder there they sing the wonder a little time to us, if we listen. Then they pass on to it. Literature is but the faint echo tangled in thousands of years, of this mighty, lonely singing of theirs,

under the Dome of Life, in the presence of the
things that books are about. The power to
read a great book is the power to glory in these
things, and to use that glory every day to do
one's living and reading with. Knowing what
is in the book may be called learning, but the
test of culture always is that it will not be content with knowledge unless it is inward knowledge. Inward knowledge is the knowledge
that comes to us from behind the book, from
living for weeks with the author until his habits
have become our habits, until God Himself,
through days and nights and deeds and dreams,
has blended our souls together.

IV

Entrance Examinations in Joy

If entrance examinations in joy were required at our representative colleges very few
of the pupils who are prepared for college in
the ordinary way would be admitted. What is
more serious than this, the honour-pupils in
the colleges themselves at commencement time
—those who have submitted most fully to the
college requirements — would take a lower
stand in a final examination in joy, whether
of sense or spirit, than any others in the class.
Their education has not consisted in the acquiring of a state of being, a condition of organs, a
capacity of tasting life, of creating and sharing

the joys and meanings in it. Their learning
has largely consisted in the fact that they have
learned at last to let their joys go. They have
become the most satisfactory of scholars, not
because of their power of knowing, but because
of their willingness to be powerless in knowing.
When they have been drilled to know without
joy, have become the day-labourers of learning, they are given diplomas for cheerlessness,
and are sent forth into the world as teachers of
the young. Almost any morning, in almost
any town or city beneath the sun, you can see
them, Gentle Reader, with the children, spreading their tired minds and their tired bodies
over all the fresh and buoyant knowledge of
the earth. Knowledge that has not been
throbbed in cannot be throbbed out. The
graduates of the colleges for women (in The
Association of Collegiate Alumnæ) have seriously discussed the question whether the college course in literature made them nearer or
farther from creating literature themselves.
The Editor of *Harper's Monthly* has recorded
that " the spontaneity and freedom of subjective
construction " in certain American authors was
only made possible, probably, by their having
escaped an early academic training. The *Century Magazine* has been so struck with the fact
that hardly a single writer of original power
before the public has been a regular college
graduate that it has offered special prizes and
inducements for any form of creative literature

—poem, story, or essay—that a college graduate could write.

If a teacher of literature desires to remove
his subject from the uncreative methods he
finds in use around him, he can only do so
successfully by persuading trustees and college
presidents that literature is an art and that it
can only be taught through the methods and
spirit and conditions that belong to art. If he
succeeds in persuading trustees and presidents,
he will probably find that faculties are not per-
suaded, and that, in the typical Germanised
institution of learning at least, any work he
may choose to do in the spirit and method of
joy will be looked upon by the larger part of
his fellow teachers as superficial and pleasant.
Those who do not feel that it is superficial and
pleasant, who grant that working for a state
of being is the most profound and worthy and
strenuous work a teacher can do,—that it is
what education is for,—will feel that it is impracticable.   It is thus that it has come to pass
in the average institution of learning, that if
a teacher does not know what education is, he
regards education as superficial, and if he does
know what education is, he regards education
as impossible.

It is not intended to be dogmatic, but it may
be worth while to state from the pupil's point
of view and from memory what kind of teacher
a college student who is really interested in
literature would like to have.

Given a teacher of literature who has *carte blanche* from the other teachers—the authorities around him—and from the trustees—the authorities over him,—what kind of a stand will he find it best to take, if he proposes to give his pupils an actual knowledge of literature?

In the first place, he will stand on the general principle that if a pupil is to have an actual knowledge of literature as literature, he must experience literature as an art.

In the second place, if he is to teach literature to his pupils as an art to be mastered, he will begin his teaching as a master. Instead of his pupils' determining that they will elect him, he will elect them. If there is to be any candidating, he will see that the candidating is properly placed; that the privilege at least of the first-class music master, dancing master, and teacher of painting—the choosing of his own pupils—is accorded to him. Inasmuch as the power and value of his class must always depend upon him, he will not allow either the size or the character of his classes to be determined by a catalogue, or by the examinations of other persons, or by the advertising facilities of the college. If actual results are to be achieved in his pupils, it can only be by his governing the conditions of their work and by keeping these conditions at all times in his own hands.

In the third place, he will see that his class

is so conducted that out of a hundred who desire to belong to it the best ten only will be
able to.

In the fourth place, he will himself not only
determine which are the best ten, but he will
make this determination on the one basis possible for a teacher of art—the basis of mutual
attraction among the pupils. He will take his
stand on the spiritual principle that if classes
are to be vital classes, it is not enough that the
pupils should elect the teacher, but the teacher
and pupils must elect each other. The basis
of an art is the mutual attraction that exists
between things that belong together. The
basis for transmitting an art to other persons
is the natural attraction that exists between
persons that belong together. The more
mutual the attraction is,—complementary or
otherwise,—the more condensed and powerful teaching can it be made the conductor of.
If a hundred candidates offer themselves, fifty
will be rejected because the attraction is not
mutual enough to insure swift and permanent
results. Out of fifty, forty will be rejected
probably for the sake of ten with whom the
mutual attraction is so great that great things
cannot help being accomplished by it.

The thorough and contagious teacher of
literature will hold his power—the power of
conveying the current and mood of art to
others—as a public trust. He owes it to the
institution in which he is placed to refuse to

surround himself with non-conductors; and inasmuch as his power—such as it is—is instinctive power, it will be placed where it instinctively counts the most. In proportion as he loves his art and loves his kind and desires to get them on speaking terms with each other, he will devote himself to selected pupils, to those with whom he will throw the least away. His service to others will be to give to these such real, inspired, and reproductive knowledge, that it shall pass on from them to others of its own inherent energy. From the narrower—that is, the less spiritual—point of view, it has seemed perhaps a selfish and aristocratic thing for a teacher to make distinctions in persons in the conduct of his work, but from the point of view of the progress of the world, it is heartless and sentimental to do otherwise; and without exception all of the most successful teachers in all of the arts have been successful quite as much through a kind of dictatorial insight in selecting the pupils they could teach, as in selecting the things they could teach them.

In the fifth place, having determined to choose his pupils himself, the selection will be determined by processes of his own choosing. These processes, whatever form or lack of form they may take, will serve to convey to the teacher the main knowledge he desires. They will be an examination in the capacity of joy in the pupil. Inasmuch as surplus joy in a pupil is the most promising thing he can have, the sole secret of any ability he may ever attain of learning literature, the basis of all discipline, it will be the first thing the teacher takes into account. While it is obvious that an examination in joy could not be conducted in any set fashion, every great joy in the world has its natural diviners and experts, and teachers of literature who know its joy have plenty of ways of divining this joy in others.

In the sixth place, pupils will be dropped and promoted by a teacher, in such a class as has been described, according to the spirit and force and creativeness of their daily work. Promotion will be by elimination—that is, the pupil will stay where he is and the class will be made smaller for him. The superior natural force of each pupil will have full sway in determining his share of the teacher's force. As this force belongs most to those who waste it least, if five tenths of the appreciation in a class belongs to one pupil, five tenths of the teacher belongs to him, and promotion is most truly effected, not by giving the best pupils a new teacher, but by giving them more of the old one. A teacher's work can only be successful in proportion as it is accurately individual and puts each pupil in the place he was made to fit.

In the seventh place, the select class will be selected by the teacher as a baseball captain selects his team: not as being the nine best men, but as being the nine men who most call each other out, and make the best play together. If the teacher selects his class wisely, the principle of his selection sometimes—from the outside, at least—will seem no principle at all. The class must have its fool, for instance, and pupils must be selected for useful defects as well as for virtues. Belonging to such a class will not be allowed to have a stiff, definite, water-metre meaning in it, with regard to the capacity of a pupil. It will only be known that he is placed in the class for some quality, fault, or inspiration in him that can be brought to bear on the state of being in the class in such a way as to produce results, not only for himself but for all concerned.

V

Natural Selection in Theory

The conditions just stated as necessary for the vital teaching of literature narrow themselves down, for the most part, to the very simple and common principle of life and art, the principle of natural selection.

As an item in current philosophy the principle of natural selection meets with general acceptance. It is one of those pleasant and instructive doctrines which, when applied to existing institutions, is opposed at once as a sensational, visionary, and revolutionary doctrine.

There are two most powerful objections to the doctrine of natural selection in education. One of these is the scholastic objection and the other is the religious one.

The scholastic objection is that natural selection in education is impracticable. It cannot be made to operate mechanically, or for large numbers, and it interferes with nearly all of the educational machinery for hammering heads in rows, which we have at command at present. Even if the machinery could be stopped and natural selection could be given the place that belongs to it, all success in acting on it would call for hand-made teachers; and hand-made teachers are not being produced when we have nothing but machines to produce them with. The scholastic objection —that natural selection in education is impracticable under existing conditions—is obviously well taken. As it cannot be answered, it had best be taken, perhaps, as a recommendation.

The religious objection to natural selection in education is not that it is impracticable, but that it is wicked. It rests its case on the defence of the weak.

But the question at issue is not whether the weak shall be served and defended or whether they shall not. We all would serve and defend the weak. If a teacher feels that he can serve his inferior pupils best by making his superior pupils inferior too, it is probable that he had better do it, and that he will know how to do it, and that he will know how to do it better than any one else. There are many teachers, however, who have the instinctive belief, and who act on it so far as they are allowed to, that to take the stand that the inferior pupil must be defended at the expense of the superior pupil is to take a sentimental stand. It is not a stand in favour of the inferior pupil, but against him.

The best way to respect an inferior pupil is to keep him in place. The more he is kept in place, the more his powers will be called upon. If he is in the place above him, he may see much that he would not see otherwise, much at which he will wonder, perhaps; but he deserves to be treated spiritually and thoroughly, to be kept where he will be creative, where his wondering will be to the point, both at once and eventually.

It is a law that holds as good in the life of a teacher of literature as it does in the lives of makers of literature. From the point of view of the world at large, the author who can do anything else has no right to write for the average man. There are plenty of people who cannot help writing for him. Let them do it. It is their right and the world's right that they should be the ones to do it. It is the place that belongs to them, and why should nearly every man we have of the more seeing kind to-day deliberately compete with men who cannot compete with him? The man who abandons the life that belongs to him,—the life that would not exist in the world if he did not live it and keep it existing in the world, and who does it to help his inferiors, does not help his inferiors. He becomes their rival. He crowds them out of their lives. There could not possibly be a more noble, or more exact and spiritual law of progress than this—that every man should take his place in human society and do his work in it with his nearest spiritual neighbours. These nearest spiritual neighbours are a part of the economy of the universe. They are now and always have been the natural conductors over the face of the earth of all actual power in it. It has been through the grouping of the nearest spiritual neighbours around the world that men have unfailingly found the heaven-appointed, world-remoulding teachers of every age.

It does not sound very much like Thomas Jefferson,—and it is to be admitted that there are certain lines in our first great national document which, read on the run at least, may seem to deny it,—but the living spirit of Thomas Jefferson does not teach that amputation is progress, nor does true Democracy admit either the patriotism or the religion of a man who feels that his legs must be cut off to run to the assistance of neighbours whose legs are cut off. An educational Democracy which expects a pupil to be less than himself

for the benefit of other pupils is a mock Democracy, and it is the very essence of a Democracy of the truer kind that it expects every
man in it to be more than himself. And if a
man's religion is of the truer kind, it will not
be heard telling him that he owes it to God
and the Average Man to be less than himself.

VI

Natural Selection in Practice

It is not going to be possible very much
longer to take it for granted that natural selection is a somewhat absent-minded and heathen
habit that God has fallen into in the natural
world, and uses in his dealings with men, but
that it is not a good enough law for men to
use in their dealings with one another.

The main thing that science has done in the
last fifty years, in spite of conventional religion
and so-called scholarship, has been to bring to
pass in men a respect for the natural world.
The next thing that is to be brought to pass—
also in spite of conventional religion and so-
called scholarship—is the self-respect of the
natural man and of the instincts of human
nature. The self-respect of the natural man,
when once he gains it, is a thing that is bound
to take care of itself, and take care of the man,
and take care of everything that is important
to the man.

Inasmuch as, in the long run at least, education, even in times of its not being human,
interests humanity more than anything else, a
most important consequence of the self-respect
of the natural man is going to be an uprising,
all over the world, of teachers who believe
something. The most important consequence
of having teachers who believe something will
be a wholesale and uncompromising rearrange-
ment of nearly all our systems and methods of
education. Instead of being arranged to cow
the teacher with routine, to keep teachers from
being human beings, and to keep their pupils
from finding it out if they are human beings,
they will be arranged on the principle that the
whole object of knowledge is the being of a
human being, and the only way to know anything worth knowing in the world is to begin
by knowing how to be a human being—and by
liking it.

Not until our current education is based
throughout on expecting great things of human
nature instead of secretly despising it, can it
truly be called education. Expectancy is the
very essence of education. Actions not only
speak louder than words, they make words as
though they were not; and so long as our
teachers confine themselves to saying beautiful
and literary things about the instincts of the
human heart, and do not trust their own instincts in their daily teaching, and the instincts
of their pupils, and do not make this trust the

foundation of all their work, the more they educate the more they destroy. The destruction is both ways, and whatever the subjects are they may choose to know, murder and suicide are the branches they teach.

The chief characteristic of the teacher of the future is going to be that he will dare to believe in himself, and that he will divine some one thing to believe in, in everybody else, and that, trusting the laws of human nature, he will go to work on this some one thing, and work out from it to everything. Inasmuch as the chief working principle of human nature is the principle of natural selection, the entire method of the teacher of the future will be based on his faith in natural selection. All such teaching as he attempts to do will be worked out from the temperamental, involuntary, primitive choices of his own being, both in persons and in subject. His power with his classes will be his power of divining the free and unconscious and primitive choices of individual pupils in persons and subjects.

Half of the battle is already won. The principle of natural selection between pupils and subjects is recognised in the elective system, but we have barely commenced to conceive as yet the principle of natural selection in its more important application—mutual attraction between teacher and pupil—natural selection in its deeper and more powerful and spiritual sense; the kind of natural selection that makes the teacher a worker in wonder, and education the handiwork of God.

In most of our great institutions we do not believe in even the theory of this deeper natural selection; and if we do believe in it, sitting in endowed chairs under the Umbrella of Endowed Ideas, how can we act on that belief? And if we do, who will come out and act with us? If it does not seem best for even the single teacher, doing his teaching unattached and quite by himself, to educate in the open,—to trust his own soul and the souls of his pupils to the nature of things, how much less shall the great institution, with its crowds of teachers and its rows of pupils and its Vested Funds be expected to lay itself open—lay its teachers and pupils and its Vested Funds open—to the nature of things? We are suspicious of the nature of things. God has concealed a lie in them. We do not believe. Therefore we cannot teach.

The conclusion is inevitable. As long as we believe in natural selection between pupil and subject, but do not believe in natural selection between pupil and teacher, no great results in education or in teaching a vital relation to books or to anything else will be possible. As long as natural selection between pupil and teacher is secretly regarded as an irreligious and selfish instinct, with which a teacher must have nothing to do, instead of a divine ordinance, a Heaven-appointed starting-point for doing everything, the average routine teacher in the conventional school and college will con-tinne to be the kind of teacher he is, and will continue to belong to what seems to many, at least, the sentimental and superstitious and pessimistic profession he belongs to now. Why should a teacher allow himself to teach without inspiration in the one profession on the earth where, between the love of God and the love of the opening faces, inspiration—one would say—could hardly be missed? Certainly, if it was ever intended that artists should be in the world it was intended that teachers should be artists. And why should we be artisans? If we cannot be artists, if we are not allowed to make our work a self-expression, were it not better to get one's living by the labour of one's hands,—by digging in the wonder of the ground? A stone-crusher, as long as one works one's will with it, makes it say something, is nearer to nature than a college. "I would rather do manual labour with my hands than manual labour with my soul," the true artist is saying to-day, and a great many thousand teachers are saying it, and thousands more who would like to teach. The moment that teaching ceases to be a trade and becomes a profession again, these thousands are going to crowd into it. Until the artist-teachers have been attracted to teaching, things can only continue as they are. Young men and women who are capable of teaching will continue to do all that they can not to get into it; and young men and women who are capable of teaching, and who are still trying to teach, will continue to do all that they can to get out of it. When the schools of America have all been obliged, like the city of Brooklyn, to advertise to secure even poor teachers, we shall begin to see where we stand,—stop our machinery a while and look at it.

The only way out is the return to nature, and to faith in the freedom of nature. Not until the teacher of the young has dared to return to nature, has won the emancipation of his own instincts and the emancipation of the instincts of his pupils, can we expect anything better than we have now of either of them. Not until the modern teacher has come to the point where he deliberately works with his instincts, where he looks upon himself as an artist working in the subject that attracts him most, and in the material that is attracted to him most, can we expect to secure in our crowded conditions to-day enough teaching to go around. The one practical and economical way to make our limited supply of passion and thought cover the ground is to be spiritual and spontaneous and thorough with what we have. The one practical and economical way to do this is to leave things free, to let the natural forces in men's lives find the places that belong to them, develop the powers that belong to them, until power in every man's life shall be contagious of power. In the meantime, having brought

out the true and vital energies of men as far as
we go, if we are obliged to be specialists in
knowledge we shall be specialists of the larger
sort. The powers of each man, being actual
and genuine powers, shall play into the powers
of other men. Each man that essays to live
shall create for us a splendour and beauty and
strength he was made to create from the beginning of the world.

To those who sit in the seat of the scornful
the somewhat lyrical idea of an examination in
joy as a basis of admission to the typical college
appeals as a fit subject of laughter. So it is.
Having admitted the laugh, the question is,—
all human life is questioning the college to-day,
—which way shall the laugh point?

If the conditions of the typical college do not
allow for the working of the laws of nature, so
much the worse for the laws of nature, or so
much the worse for the college. In the meantime, it is good to record that there are many
signs—thanks to these same laws of nature—
that a most powerful reaction is setting in, not
only in the colleges themselves, but in all the
forces of culture outside and around them.
The examination in joy—the test of natural selection—is already employed by all celebrated
music masters the world over in the choosing
of pupils, and by all capable teachers of painting; and the time is not far off when, so far as
courses in literature are concerned (if the
teaching of literature is attempted in crowded

institutions), the examination in joy will be the determining factor with all the best teachers, not only in the conduct of their classes, but in the very structure of them. Structure is the basis of conduct.

VII

The Emancipation of the Teacher

The custom of mowing lawns in cities, of having every grass-blade in every door-yard like every other grass-blade, is considered by many persons as an artificial custom—a violation of the law of nature. It is contended that the free-swinging, wind-blown grasses of the fields are more beautiful and that they give more various and infinite delight in colour and line and movement. If a piece of this same field, however, could be carefully cut out and moved and fitted to a city door-yard—bobolinks and daisies and shadows and all, precisely as they are — it would not be beautiful. Long grass conforms to a law of nature where nature has room, and short grass conforms to a law of nature where nature has not room.

When, for whatever reason, of whatever importance, men and women choose to be so close together, that it is not fitting they should have freedom, and when they choose to have so little room to live in that development is not fitting lest it should inconvenience others, the penalty follows. When grass-blades are crowded between walls and fences, the more they can be made to look alike the more pleasing they are, and when an acre of ground finds itself covered with a thousand people, or a teacher of culture finds himself mobbed with pupils, the law of nature is the same. Whenever crowding of any kind takes place, whether it be in grass, ideas, or human nature, the most pleasing as well as the most convenient and natural way of producing a beautiful effect is with the Lawn Mower. The dead level is the logic of crowded conditions. The city grades down its hills for the convenience of reducing its sewer problem. It makes its streets into blocks for the convenience of knowing where every home is, and how far it is, by a glance at a page, and, in order that the human beings in it (one set of innumerable nobodies hurrying to another set of innumerable nobodies) may never be made to turn out perchance for an elm on a sidewalk, it cuts down centuries of trees, and then, out of its modern improvements, its map of life, its woods in rows, its wheels on tracks, and its souls in pigeonholes — out of its huge Checker-board under the days and nights—it lifts its eyes to the smoke in heaven, at last, and thanks God it is civilised !

The substantial fact in the case would seem to be that every human being born into the world has a right to be treated as a special creation all by himself. Society can only be said to be truly civilised in proportion as it acts on this fact. It is because in the family each being is treated as one out of six or seven, and in the school as one out of six hundred, that the family (with approximately good parents) comes nearer to being a model school than anything we have.

If we deliberately prefer to live in crowds for the larger part of our lives, we must expect our lives to be cut and fitted accordingly. It is an æsthetic as well as a practical law that this should be so. The law of nature where there is room for a man to be a man is not the law of nature where there is not room for him to be a man. If there is no playground for his individual instincts except the street he must give them up. Inasmuch as natural selection in overcrowded conditions means selecting things by taking them away from others, it can be neither beautiful nor useful to practise it.

People who prefer to be educated in masses must conform to the law of mass, which is inertia, and to the law of the herd, which is the Dog. As long as our prevailing idea of the best elective is the one with the largest class, and the prevailing idea of culture is the degree from the most crowded college, all natural gifts, whether in teachers or pupils, are under a penalty. If we deliberately place ourselves where everything is done by the gross, as a

matter of course and in the nature of things
the machine-made man, taught by the machine-
made teacher, in a teaching-machine, will continue to be the typical scholar of the modern
world; and the gentleman-scholar — the man
who made himself, or who gave God a chance
to make him—will continue to be what he is
now in most of our large teaching communities
—an exception.

Culture which has not the power to win the
emancipation of its teachers does not produce
emancipated and powerful pupils. The essence
of culture is selection, and the essence of selection is natural selection, and teachers who
have not been educated with natural selection
cannot teach with it. Teachers who have
given up being individuals in the main activity
of their lives, who are not allowed to be individuals in their teaching, do not train pupils to
be individuals. Their pupils, instead of being
organic human beings, are manufactured ones.
Literary drill in college consists in drilling
every man to be himself—in giving him the
freedom of himself. Probably it would be admitted by most of us who are college graduates
that the teachers who loom up in our lives
are those whom we remember as emancipated
teachers—men who dared to be individuals in
their daily work, and who, every time they
touched us, helped us to be individuals.

VIII

The Test of Culture

Looking at our great institutions of learning in a general way, one might be inclined to feel that literature cannot be taught in them, because the classes are too large. When one considers, however, the average class in literature, as it actually is, and the things that are being taught in it, it becomes obvious that the larger such a class can be made, and the less the pupil can be made to get out of it, the better.

The best test of a man's knowledge of the Spanish language would be to put him in a balloon and set him down in dark night in the middle of Spain and leave him there with his Spanish words. The best test of a man's knowledge of books is to see what he can do without them on a desert island in the sea. When the ship's library over the blue horizon dwindles at last in its cloud of smoke and he is left without a shred of printed paper by him, the supreme opportunity of education will come to him. He will learn how vital and beautiful, or boastful and empty, his education is. If it is true education, the first step he takes he will find a use for it. The first bird that floats from its tree-top shall be a message from London straight to his soul. If he has truly known them, the spirits of all his books will flock to him. If he has known Shake-

speare, the ghost of the great master will rise
from beneath its Stratford stone, and walk
oceans to be with him. If he knows Homer,
Homer is full of Odysseys trooping across the
seas. Shall he sit him down on the rocks, lift
his voice like a mere librarian, and, like a
book-raised, paper-pampered, ink-hungry babe
cry to the surf for a Greek dictionary? The
rhythm of the beach is Greece to him, and the
singing of the great Greek voice is on the tops
of waves around the world.

A man's culture is his knowledge become
himself. It is in the seeing of his eyes and the
hearing of his ears and the use of his hands.
Is there not always the altar of the heavens
and the earth? Laying down days and nights
of joy before it and of beauty and wonder and
peace, the scholar is always a scholar, *i. e.*, he
is always at home. To be cultured is to be so
splendidly wrought of body and soul as to get
the most joy out of the least and the fewest
things. Wherever he happens to be,—whatever he happens to be without,—his culture is
his being master. He may be naked before
the universe, and it may be a pitiless universe
or a gracious one, but he is always master,
knowing how to live in it, knowing how to
hunger and die in it, or, like Stevenson, smiling
out of his poor, worn body to it. He is the
unconquerable man. Wherever he is in the
world, he cannot be old in the presence of
the pageant of Life. From behind the fading

of his face he watches it, child after child, spring after spring as it flies before him; he will not grow old while it still passes by. It carries delight across to him to the end. He watches and sings with it to the end, down to the edge of sleep.

A bird's shadow is enough to be happy with, if a man is educated, or the flicker of light on a leaf, and when really a song is being lived in a man, all nature plays its accompaniment. To possess one's own senses, to know how to conduct one's self, is to be the conductor of orchestras in the clouds and in the grass. The trained man is not dependent on having the thing itself. He borrows the boom of the sea to live with, anywhere, and the gladness of continents.

Literary training consists in the acquiring of a state of mind and body to feel the universe with; in becoming an athlete toward beauty, a giver of great lifts of joy to this poor, straining, stumbling world with its immemorial burden on its back, which, going round and round, for the most part with its eyes shut, between infinities, is the hope and sorrow of all of us for the very reason that its eyes are shut.

IX

Summary

The proper conditions for literary drill in college would seem to sum themselves up in the general idea that literature is the spirit of life. It can therefore only be taught through the spirit.

First. It can only be taught through the spirit by being taught as an art, through its own nature and activity, reproductively—giving the spirit body. Both the subject-matter and the method in true literary drill can only be based on the study of human experience. The intense study of human experience in a college course may be fairly said to involve three things that must be daily made possible to the pupil in college life. Everything that is given him to do, and everything that happens to him in college, should cultivate these three things in the pupil: (1) Personality—an intense first person singular, as a centre for having experience; (2) Imagination — the natural organ in the human soul for realising what an experience is and for combining and condensing it; (3) The habit of having time and room, for re-experiencing an experience at will in the imagination, until the experience becomes so powerful and vivid, so fully realises itself in the mind, that the owner of the mind is an artist with his mind. When he puts the experience of his mind down it becomes more real to other men on paper than their own experiences are to them in their own lives.

It is hardly necessary to point out that whatever our conventional courses in literature may be doing, whether in college or anywhere else,

Summary

they are not bringing out this creative joy and habit of creative joy in the pupils. Those who are interested in literature-courses—such as we have—for the most part do not believe in trying to bring out the creative joy of each pupil. Those who might believe in trying to do it do not believe it can be done. They do not believe it can be done because they do not realise that in the case of each and every pupil —so far as he goes—it is the only thing worth doing. They fail to see from behind their commentaries and from out of their footnotes, the fact that the one object in studying literature is joy, that the one way of studying and knowing literature is joy, and that the one way to attain joy is to draw out creative joy.

Second. And if literature is to be taught as an art it must be taught as a way of life. As long as literature and life continue to be conceived and taught as being separate things, there can be no wide and beautiful hope for either of them. The organs of literature are precisely the same organs and they are trained on precisely the same principles as the organs of life.

Except an education in books can bring to pass the right condition of these organs, a state of being in the pupil, his knowledge of no matter how long a list of masterpieces is but a catalogue of the names of things for ever left out of his life. It is little wonder, when the drudgery has done its work and the sorry show is over, and the victim of the System is face to face with his empty soul at last, if in his earlier years at least he seems overfond to some of us of receiving medals, honours, and valedictories for what he might have been and of flourishing a Degree for what he has missed.

> There was once a Master of Arts,
> Who was " nuts " upon cranberry tarts:
>   When he 'd eaten his fill
>   He was awfully ill,
> But he was still a Master of Arts.

The power and habit of studying and enjoying human nature as it lives around us, is not only a more human and alive occupation, but it is a more literary one than becoming another editor of Æschylus or going down to posterity in footnotes as one of the most prominent bores that Shakespeare ever had. If a teacher of literature enjoys being the editor of Æschylus, or if he is happier in appearing on a title-page with a poet than he could possibly be in being a poet, it is personally well enough, though it may be a disaster to the rest of us and to Æschylus. Men who can be said as a class to care more about literature than they do about life, who prefer the paper side of things to the real one, are at liberty as private persons to be editors and footnote hunters to the top of their bent; but why should they call it " The Study of Literature," to teach their pupils to be footnote hunters and editors? and how can they possibly teach anything else? and do they teach anything else? And if good teachers can only teach what they have, what shall we expect of poor ones?

In the meantime the Manufacture of the Cultured Mind is going ruthlessly on, and thousands of young men and women who, left alone with the masters of literature, might be engaged in accumulating and multiplying inspiration, are engaged in analysing—dividing what inspiration they have; and, in the one natural, creative period of their lives, their time is entirely spent in learning how inspired work was done, or how it might have been done, or how it should have been done; in absorbing everything about it except its spirit— the power that did it—the power that makes being told how to do it uncalled for, the power that asks and answers its " Hows ? " for itself. The serene powerlessness of it all, without courage or passion or conviction, without self-discovery in it, or self-forgetfulness or beauty in it, or for one moment the great contagion of the great, is one of the saddest sights in this modern day.

In the meantime the most practical thing that can be done with the matter of literary drill in college is to turn the eye of the public on it. Methods will change when ideals change, and ideals will change when the public clearly sees ideals, and when the public encourages colleges that see them. The time is not far off when it will be admitted by all concerned that the true study of masterpieces consists, and always must consist, in communing with the things that masterpieces are about, in the learning and applying of the principles of human nature, in a passion for real persons, and in a daily loving of the face of the universe.

This idea may not be considered very practical. It stands for a kind of education in which it is difficult to exhibit in rows actual results. We are not contending for an education that looks practical. We are contending merely for education that will be true and beautiful and natural. It will be practical the way the forces of nature are practical—whether any one notices it or not.

The following announcement can already be seen on the bulletin boards of universities around the world(—if looked for twice).

THEY ARE COMING ! O Shades of Learning, THE LOVERS OF JOY, IMPERIOUS WITH JOY, UNCONQUERABLE !

Their Sails are Flocking the East.

The High Seas are Theirs.

They shall command you, overwhelm you. Book-lubbers, paper-plodders, shall be as though they were not. The youth of the earth shall be renewed in the morning, the suns and the stars shall be unlocked, and the evening shall go forth with joy. The mountains shall be freed from the pick and the shovel and the book, and lift themselves

to heaven. Flowers shall again outblossom
botanies, and gymnasts of music shall be laid
low, and Birds Through An Opera Glass shall
sing. Joy shall come to knowledge, and the
strength of Joy upon it. THEY ARE COMING,
O Ye Shades of Learning, a thousand thousand strong. Their sails flock the Sea. The
smoke and the throb of their engines is the
promise of the east. The days of thirteen-
thousand-ton, three-horse-power education are
numbered.

X

A Note

It is one of the danger signs of the times that
the men who have most closely observed our
modern life, in its social, industrial, artistic,
educational, and religious aspects seem to be
gradually coming to the point where they all
but take it for granted in considering all social,
industrial, and educational and political questions, that the conditions of modern times are
such, and are going to be such that imagination and personality might as well be dropped
as practical forces—forces that must be reck-
oned with in the movement of human life.
Nearly all the old-time outlooks of the Soul,
as they stand in history, have been taken for
factory sites, bought up by syndicates, moral
and otherwise, and are being used for chim-

neys. Nothing but smoke and steel and wooden Things come out of them. Poets and brokers are both telling us on every hand that imagination is impossible and personality incredible in modern life.

Imagination and personality are the spirit and the dust out of which all great nations and all great religions are made.

The attempt has been made in the foregoing pages to point out that they are not dead. The Altar smoulders.

In pointing out how imagination and personality can be wrought into one single branch of a man's education—his relation to books—principles may have been suggested which can be concretely applied by all of us, each in our own department, to the education of the whole man.

Part II

Possibilities

I

The Issue

I DREAMED I lived in a day when men dared have visions. I lay in a great white Silence as one who waited for something.

And as I lay and waited, the Silence groped toward me and I felt it gathering nearer and nearer about me.

Then it folded me to Itself.

I made Time my bedside.

And it seemed to me, when I had rested my soul with years, and when I had found Space and had stretched myself upon it, I awoke.

I lay in a great white empty place, and the whole world like solemn music came to me.

And I looked, and behold in the shadow of the earth, which came and went, I saw Human Lives being tossed about. On the solemn rhythmic music, back and forth, I saw them lifted across Silence.

And I said to my Spirit, "What is it they are doing?"

" They are living," the Spirit said.

So they floated before me while The Great Shadow came and went.

.   .   .   .

O my Soul, hast thou forgotten thy days in the world, when thou didst watch the processional of it, when the faces — day-lighted, night-lighted, faces—trooped before thee, and thou didst look upon them and delight in them ? What didst thou see in the world ? "

" I saw Two Immeasurable Hands in it," said my Soul, " over every man. I saw that the man did not see the Hands. I saw that they reached out of infinity for him down through the days and the nights. And whether he slept or prayed or wrought, I saw that they still reached out for him, and folded themselves about him."

And I asked God what The Hands were.

" The man calls them Heredity and Environment," God said.

And God laughed.

Words came from far for me and waited in tumult within me. But my mouth was filled with silence.

.   .   .   .

I know that I do not know the world, but out of my little corner of time and space I have watched in it,—watched men and truths struggling in it, and in the struggle it has seemed to me I have seen three kinds of men. I have seen the man who feels that he is being made, and the man who feels that he is making himself. But I have seen also another kind of man—the man who feels that the Universe is at work on him, but (within limits) under his own supervision.

I have made a compact in my soul with this man, for a new world. He is not willing to be a mere manufactured man—one more being turned out from The Factory of Circumstance—neither does he think very much of the man who makes himself—who could make himself. If he were to try such a thing—try to make a man himself, he would really rather try it, if the truth must be told, on some one else.

As near as he can define it, life seems to be (to the normal or inspired man) a kind of alternate grasping and being grasped. Sometimes he feels his destiny tossed between the Two Immeasurable Hands. Sometimes he feels that they have paused—that the Immeasurable Hands have been lent to him, that the toss of destiny is made his own.

He watches these two great forces playing under heaven, before his eyes, with his immortal life, every day. His soul takes these powers of heaven, as the mariner takes the winds of the sea. He tacks to destiny. He takes the same attitude toward the laws of heredity and environment that the Creator took when He made them. He takes it for granted that a God who made these laws as

conveniences for Himself, in running a Universe, must have intended them for men as
conveniences in living in it.   In proportion as
men have been like God they have treated
these laws as He does—as conveniences.
Thousands of men are doing it to-day.   Men
did it for thousands of years before they knew
what the laws were, when they merely followed their instincts with them.   In a man's
answer to the question, How can I make a
convenience of the law of heredity and environment?—education before being born and education after being born—will be found to lie
always the secret glory or the secret shame of
his life.

II

The First Selection

If the souls of the unborn could go about
reconnoitering the earth a little before they
settled on it, selecting the parents they would
have, the places where it pleased them to be
born, nine out of ten of them (judging from
the way they conduct themselves in the flesh)
would spend nearly all their time in looking
for the best house and street to be born in,
the best things to be born to.   Such a little
matter as selecting the right parents would be
left, probably, to the last moment, or they
would expect it to be thrown in.

We are all of us more or less aware, es-

pecially as we advance in life, that overlook-
ing the importance of parents is a mistake.
There have been times in the lives of some of
us when having parents at all seemed a mistake. We can remember hours when we were
sure we had the wrong ones. After our first dis-
appointment,—that is, when we have learned
how unmanageable parents are,—we have our
time—most of us—of making comparisons, of
trying other people's parents on. This cannot
be said to work very well, taken as a whole,
and it is generally admitted that people who
are most serious about it, who take unto themselves fathers- and mothers-in-law seldom do
any better than at first. The conclusion of the
whole matter would seem to be: Since a man
cannot select his parents and his parents cannot select him, he must select himself.

That is what books are for.

III

Conveniences

It is the first importance of a true book that
a man can select his neighbours with it,—can
overcome space, riches, poverty, and time with
it,—and the grave, and break bread with the
dead. A book is a portable miracle. It
makes a man's native place all over for him,
for a dollar and a quarter; and many a man in
this somewhat hard and despairing world has

been furnished with a new heaven and a new
earth for twenty-five cents. Out of a public
library he has felt reached down to him the
grasp of heroes. Hurrying home in the night,
perhaps, with his tiny life hid under stars,
but with a Book under his arm, he has felt a
Greeting against his breast and held it tight.
" Who art thou, my lad ? " it said; " who art
thou ? " And the saying was not forgotten.
If it is true that the spirits of the mighty dead
are abroad in the night they are turning the
leaves of books.

There are other inspiring things in the
world, but there is nothing else that carries
itself among the sons of men like the book.
With such divine plenteousness—seeds of the
worlds in it—it goes about flocking on the
souls of men. There is something so broad-
cast, so universal about the way of a book with
a man: boundless, subtle, ceaseless, irresistible,
following him and loving him, renewing him,
delighting in him and hoping for him—like a
god. It is as the way of Nature herself with
a man. One cannot always feel it, but somehow, when I am really living a real day, I feel
as if some Great Book were around me—were
always around me. I feel myself all-enfolded,
penetrated, surrounded with it — the vast,
gentle force of it—sky and earth of it. It is as
if I saw it, sometimes, building new boundaries
for me, out there—softly, gently, on the edges
of the night—for me and for all human life.

Other inspiring things seem to be less stead-
fast for us. They cannot always free themselves and then come and free us. Music
cannot be depended upon. It sings sometimes
for and sometimes against us. Sometimes,
also, music is still—absolutely still, all the way
down from the stars to the grass. At best it is
for some people and for others not, and is ad-
dicted to places. It is a part of the air—part
of the climate in Germany, but there is but
one country in the world made for listening in
—where any one, every one listens, the way
one breathes. The great pictures inspire, on
the whole, but few people—most of them with
tickets. Cathedrals cannot be unmoored, have
never been seen by the majority of men at
all, except in dreams and photographs. Most
mountains (for all practical purposes) are
private property. The sea (a look at the
middle of it) is controlled by two or three
syndicates. The sky—the last stronghold of
freedom — is rented out for the most part,
where most men live—in cities; and in New
York and London the people who can afford
it pay taxes for air, and grass is a dollar a
blade. Being born is the only really free thing
—and dying. Next to these in any just estimate of the comparatively free raw material
that goes to the making of a human life comes
the printed book.

A library, on the whole, is the purest and
most perfect form of power that exists, because

it is a lever on the nature of things. If a man is born with the wrong neighbours it brings the right ones flocking to him. It is the universe to order. It makes the world like a globe in a child's hands. He turns up the part where he chooses to live—now one way and now another, that he may delight in it and live in it. If he is a poet it is the meaning of life to him that he can keep on turning it until he has delighted and tasted and lived in all of it.

The second importance of true books is that they are not satisfied with the first. They are not satisfied to be used to influence a man from the outside—as a kind of house-furnishing for his soul. A true book is never a mere contrivance for arranging the right bit of sky for a man to live his life under, or the right neighbours for him to live his life with. It goes deeper than this. A mere playing upon a man's environment does not seem to satisfy a true book. It plays upon the latent infinity in the man himself. The majority of men are not merely conceived in sin and born in lies, but they are the lies; and lies as well as truths flow in their veins. Lies hold their souls back thousands of years. When one considers the actual facts about most men, the law of environment seems a clumsy and superficial law enough. If all that a book can do is to appeal to the law of environment for a man, it does not do very much. The very trees and stones do better for him, and the little birds in their

nests.　No possible amount of environment
crowded on their frail souls would ever make
it possible for most men to catch up—to overtake enough truth before they die to make
their seventy years worth while.　The majority
of men (one hardly dares to deny) can be seen,
sooner or later, drifting down to death either
bitterly or indifferently.　The shadows of their
lives haunt us a little, then they vanish away
from us and from the sound of our voices.
Oh, God, from behind Thy high heaven—from
out of Thy infinite wealth of years, hast Thou
but the one same pittance of threescore and
ten for every man ?　Some of us are born with
the handicap of a thousand years woven in the
nerves of our bodies, the swiftness of our
minds, and the delights of our limbs.　Others
of us are born with the thousand years binding
us down to blindness and hobbling, holding us
back to disease, but all with the same Imperious Timepiece held above us, to run the same
race, to overtake the same truth—before the
iron curtain and the dark.　Some of us—a few
men in every generation—have two or three
hundred years given to us outright the day we
are born.　Then we are given seventy more.
Others of us have two hundred years taken
away from us the day we are born.　Then we
are given seventy years to make them up in,
and it is called life.

If we are to shut ourselves up with one law,
either the law of environment or the law of

heredity, it is obvious that the best a logical man could do, would be to be ashamed of a universe like this and creep out of it as soon as he could. The great glory of a great book is, that it will not let itself be limited to the law of environment in dealing with a man. It deals directly with the man himself. It appeals to the law of heredity. It reaches down into the infinite depth of his life. If a man has started a life with parents he had better not have (for all practical purposes), it furnishes him with better ones. It picks and chooses in behalf of his life out of his very grandfathers, for him. It not only supplies him with a new set of neighbours as often as he wants them. It sees that he is born again every morning on the wide earth and that he has a new set of parents to be born to. It is a part of the infinite and irrepressible hopefulness of this mortal life that each man of us who dwells on the earth is the child of an infinite marriage. We are all equipped, even the poorest of us, from the day we begin, with an infinite number of fathers and an infinite number of mothers—no telling, as we travel down the years, which shall happen to us next. If what we call heredity were a matter of a few months,—a narrow, pitiful, two-parent affair,— if the fate of a human being could be shut in with what one man and one woman, playing and working, eating and drinking, under heaven, for a score of years or more, would be likely to have to give him from out of their very selves, heredity would certainly be a whimsical, unjust, undignified law to come into a world by, to don an immortal soul with. A man who has had his life so recklessly begun for him could hardly be blamed for being reckless with it afterward. But it is not true that the principle of heredity in a human life can be confined to a single accident in it. We are all infinite, and our very accidents are infinite. In the very flesh and bones of our bodies we are infinite — brought from the furthest reaches of eternity and the utmost bounds of created life to be ourselves. If we were to do nothing else for threescore years, it is not in our human breath to recite our fathers' names upon our lips. Each of us is the child of an infinite mother, and from her breast, veiled in a thousand years, we draw life, glory, sorrow, sleep, and death. The ones we call fathers and mothers are but ambassadors to us—delegates from a million graves—appointed for our birth. Every boy is a summed-up multitude. The infinite crowd of his fathers beckons for him. As in some vast amphitheatre he lives his life, before the innumerable audience of the dead—each from its circle of centuries—calls to him, contends for him, draws him to himself.

Inasmuch as every man who is born in the world is born with an infinite outfit for living in it, it is the office of all books that are true and

beautiful books—true to the spirit of a man—
that they shall play upon the latent infinity in
him; that they shall help him to select his
largest self; that they shall help him to give,
as the years go on, the right accent to the right
fathers, in his life.

Books are more close to the latent infinity in
a human being than anything else can be, because the habit of the infinite is their habit.
As books are more independent of space and
time than all other known forces in the lives
of men, they seem to make all the men who
love them independent also. If a man has not
room for his life, he takes a book and makes
room for it. When the habit of books becomes
the habit of a man he unhands himself at will
from space and time; he finds the universe is
his universe. He finds ancestors and neighbours alike flocking to him—doing his bidding.
God Himself says " Yes " to him and delights
in him. He has entered into conspiracy with
the nature of things. He does not feel that he
is being made. He does not feel that he is
making himself. The universe is at work on
him—under his own supervision.

IV

The Charter of Possibility

In reading to select one's parents and one's
self, there seem to be two instincts involved.

These instincts may vary more or less according to the book and the mood of the reader, but the object of all live reading—of every live experience with a book—is the satisfying of one or both of them. A man whose reading means something to him is either letting himself go in a book or letting himself come in it. He is either reading himself out or reading himself in. It is as if every human life were a kind of port on the edge of the universe, when it reads, — possible selves outward - bound and inward-bound trooping before It. Some of these selves are exports and some are imports.

If the principle of selection is conceived in a large enough spirit, and is set in operation soon enough, and is continued long enough, there is not a child that can be born on the earth who shall not be able to determine by the use of books, in the course of the years, what manner of man he shall be. He may not be able to determine how soon he shall be that man, or how much of that man shall be fulfilled in himself before he dies, and how much of him shall be left over to be fulfilled in his children, but the fact remains that to an extraordinary degree, through a live use of books, not only a man's education after he is born, but his education before he is born, is placed in his hands. It is the supreme office of books that they do this; that they place the laws of heredity and environment where a man with a determined spirit can do something besides cringing to them. Neither environment nor heredity — taken by itself—can give a man a determined spirit, but it is everything to know that, given a few books and the determined spirit both, a man can have any environment he wants for living his life, and his own assorted ancestors for living it. It is only by means of books that a man can keep from living a partitioned-off life in the world—can keep toned up to the divine sense of possibility in it. We hear great men every day, across space and time, halloaing to one another in books, and across all things, as we feel and read, is the call of our possible selves. Even the impossible has been achieved, books tell us, in history, again and again. It has been achieved by several men. This may not prove very much, but if it does not prove anything else, it proves that the possible, at least, is the privilege of the rest of us. It has its greeting for every man. The sense of the possible crowds around him, and not merely in his books nor merely in his life, but in the place where his life and books meet —in his soul. However or wherever a man may be placed, it is the great book that re-minds him Who he is. It reminds him who his Neighbour is. It is his charter of possibility. Having seen, he acts on what he sees, and reads himself out and reads himself in accordingly.

V

The Great Game

It would be hard to say which is the more important, reading for exports or imports, reading one's self out or reading one's self in, but inasmuch as the importance of reading one's self out is more generally overlooked, it may be well to dwell upon it. Most of the reading theories of the best people to-day, judging from the prohibitions of certain books, overlook the importance altogether, in vital and normal persons — especially the young, — of reading one's self out. It is only as some people keep themselves read out, and read out regularly, that they can be kept from bringing evil on the rest of us. If Eve had had a novel, she would have sat down under the Tree and read about the fruit instead of eating it. If Adam had had a morning paper, he would hardly have listened to his wife's suggestion. If the Evil One had come up to Eve in the middle of *Les Miserables*, or one of Rossetti's sonnets, no one would ever have heard of him. The main misfortune of Adam and Eve was that they had no arts to come to the rescue of their religion. If Eve could have painted the apple, she would not have eaten it. She put it into her mouth because she could not think of anything else to do with it, and she had to do something. She had the artistic temperament (inherited from her mother Sleep, probably, or from being born in a dream), and the temptation of the artistic temperament is, that it gets itself expressed or breaks something. She had tried everything — flowers, birds, clouds, and her shadow in the stream, but she found they were all inexpressible. She could not express them. She could not even express herself. Taking walks in Paradise and talking with the one man the place afforded was not a complete and satisfying self-expression. Adam had his limitations—like all men. There were things that could not be said.

Standing as we do on the present height of history, with all the resources of sympathy in the modern world, its countless arts drawing the sexes together, going about understanding people, communing with them, and expressing them, making a community for every man, even in his solitude, it is not hard to see that the comparative failure of the first marriage was a matter of course. The real trouble was that Adam and Eve, standing in their brand-new world, could not express themselves to one another. As there was nothing else to express them, they were bored. It is to Eve's credit that she was more bored than Adam was, and that she resented it more; and while a Fall, under the circumstances, was as painful as it was inevitable, and a rather extreme measure on Eve's part, no one will deny that it afforded relief on the main point. It seems

to be the universal instinct of all Eve's sons
and daughters that have followed since, that an
expressive world is better than a dull one.
An expressive world is a world in which all
the men and women are getting themselves
expressed, either in their experiences or in
their arts—that is, in other people's experiences.

The play, the picture, and the poem and the
novel and the symphony have all been the outgrowth of Eve's infinity. She could not contain herself. She either had more experience
than she could express, or she had more to
express than she could possibly put into experience.

One of the worst things that we know about
the Japanese is that they have no imperative
mood in the language. To be able to say of a
nation that it has been able to live for thousands of years without feeling the need of an
imperative, is one of the most terrible and
sweeping accusations that has ever been made
against a people on the earth. Swearing may
not be respectable, but it is a great deal more
respectable than never wanting to. Either a
man is dead in this world, or he is out looking
for words on it. There is a great place left
over in him, and as long as that place is left
over, it is one of the practical purposes of
books to make it of some use to him. Whether
the place is a good one or a bad one, something
must be done with it, and books must do it.

If there were wordlessness for five hundred years, man would seek vast inarticulate words for himself. Cathedrals would rise from the ground undreamed as yet to say we worshipped. Music would be the daily necessity of the humblest life. Orchestras all around the world would be created, — would float language around the dumbness in it. Composers would become the greatest, the most practical men in all the nations. Viaducts would stretch their mountains of stone across the valleys to find a word that said we were strong. Out of the stones of the hills, the mists of rivers, out of electricity, even out of silence itself, we would force expression. From the time a baby first moves his limbs to when—an old man—he struggles for his last breath, the one imperious divine necessity of life is expression. Hence the artist now and for ever—the ruler of history—whoever makes it. And if he cannot make it, he makes the makers of it. The artist is the man who, failing to find neighbours for himself, makes his neighbours with his own hands. If a woman is childless, she paints Madonnas. It is the inspiration, the despair that rests over all life. If we cannot express ourselves in things that are made, we make things, and if we cannot express ourselves in the things we make, we turn to words, and if we cannot express ourselves in words, we turn to other men's words.

The man who is satisfied with one life does

not exist. The suicide does not commit suicide because he is tired of life, but because he wants so many more lives that he cannot have. The native of the tropics buys a book to the North Pole. If we are poor, we grow rich on paper. We roll in carriages through the highway of letters. If we are rich, we revel in a printed poverty. We cry our hearts out over our starving paper-children and hold our shivering, aching magazine hands over dying coals in garrets we live in by subscription at three dollars a year. The Bible is the book that has influenced men most in the world because it has expressed them the most. The moment it ceases to be the most expressive book, it will cease to be the most practical and effective one in human life. There is more of us than we can live. The touch of the infinite through which our spirits wandered is still upon us. The world cries to the poet: " Give me a new word—a word—a word! I will have a word!" It cries to the great man out of all its narrow places: " Give me another life! I will have a new life!" and every hero the world has known is worn threadbare with worship, because his life says for other men what their lives have tried to say. Every masterful life calls across the world a cry of liberty to pent-up dreams, to the ache of faith in all of us, " Here thou art my brother—this is thy heart that I have lived." A hero is immortalised because his life is every man's larger self. So through the day-span of our years—a tale that is never told—we wander on, the infinite heart of each of us prisoned in blood and flesh and the cry of us everywhere, throughout all being, "Give me room!" It cries to the composer, "Make a high wide place for me!" and on the edge of the silence between life and words, to music we come at last because it is the supreme confidante of the human heart, the confessional, the world-priest between the actual self and the larger self of all of us. With all the multiplying of arts and the piling up of books that have come to us, the most important experience that men have had in this world since they began on it, is that they are infinite, that they cannot be expressed on it. It is not infrequently said that men must get themselves expressed in living, but the fact remains that no one has ever heard of a man as yet who really did it, or who was small enough to do it. There was One who seemed to express Himself by living and by dying both, but if He had any more than succeeded in beginning to express Himself, no one would have believed that He was the Son of God,—even that He was the Son of Man. It was because He could not crowd all that He was into thirty-three short years and twelve disciples and one Garden of Gethsemane and one Cross that we know who He was.

Riveted down to its little place with iron circumstance, the actual self in every man depends upon the larger possible self for the something that makes the actual self worth while. It is hard to be held down by circumstance, but it would be harder to be contented there, to live without those intimations of our diviner birth that come to us in books—books that weave some of the glory we have missed in our actual lives, into the glory of our thoughts. Even if life be to the uttermost the doing of what are called practical things, it is only by the occasional use of his imagination in reading or otherwise, that the practical man can hope to be in physical or mental condition to do them. He needs a rest from his actual self. A man cannot even be practical without this imaginary or larger self. Unless he can work off his unexpressed remnant, his limbs are not free. Even down to the meanest of us, we are incurably larger than anything we can do.

Reading a book is a game a man plays with his own infinity.

VI

𝔒𝔲𝔱𝔴𝔞𝔯𝔡 𝔅𝔬𝔲𝔫𝔡

If there could only be arranged some mystical place over the edge of human existence, where we all could go and practise at living, have full-dress rehearsals of our parts, before we are hustled in front of the footlights in our very

swaddling clothes, how many people are there
who have reached what are fabulously called
years of discretion, who would not believe in
such a place, and who would not gladly go
back to it and spend most of the rest of their
lives there?

This is one of the things that the world of
books is for. Most of us would hardly know
what to do without it, the world of books, if
only as a place to make mistakes and to feel
foolish in. It seems to be the one great un-
observed retreat, where all the sons of men
may go, may be seen flocking day and night,
to get the experiences they would not have,
to be ready for those they cannot help having. It is the Rehearsal Room of History.
The gods watch it—this Place of Books—as we
who live go silent, trooping back and forth in
it—the ceaseless, heartless, awful, beautiful
pantomime of life.

It seems to be the testimony of human nature, after a somewhat immemorial experience,
that some things in us had better be expressed
by being lived, and that other things had better
be expressed—if possible—in some other way.

There are a great many men, even amongst
the wisest and strongest of us, who benefit every
year of their lives by what might be called the
purgative function of literature,—men who, if
they did not have a chance at the right moment to commit certain sins with their imaginary selves, would commit them with their real

ones. Many a man of the larger and more comprehensive type, hungering for the heart of all experience, bound to have its spirit, if not itself, has run the whole gamut of his possible selves in books, until all the sins and all the songs of men have coursed through his being. He finds himself reading not only to fill his lungs with ozone and his heart with the strength of the gods, but to work off the humour in his blood, to express his underself, and get it out of the way. Women who never cry their tears out—it is said—are desperate, and men who never read their sins away are dangerous. People who are tired of doing wrong on paper do right. To be sick of one's sins in a book saves not only one's self but every one else a deal of trouble. A man has not learned how to read until he reads with his veins as well as his arteries.

It would be useless to try to make out that evil passions in literature accomplish any absolute good, but they accomplish a relative good which the world can by no means afford to overlook. The amount of crime that is suggested by reading can be more than offset by the extraordinary amount of crime waiting in the hearts of men, aimed at the world and glanced off on paper.

There are many indications that this purgative function of literature is the main thing it is for in our present modern life. Modern life is so constituted that the majority of people who live in it are expressing their real selves more truly in their reading than they are in their lives. When one stops to consider what these lives are—most of them —there can be but one conclusion about the reading of the people who have to live them, and that is that while sensational reading may be an evil, as compared with the evil that has made it necessary, it is an immeasurable blessing.

The most important literary and artistic fact of the nineteenth century is the subdivision of labour—that is, the subdividing of every man's life and telling him he must only be alive in a part of it. In proportion as an age takes sensations out of men's lives it is obliged to put them into their literature. Men are used to sensations on the earth as long as they stay on it and they are bound to have them in one way or another. An age which narrows the actual lives of men, which so adjusts the labour of the world that nearly every man in it not only works with a machine, spiritual or otherwise, but is a machine himself, and a small part of a machine, must not find fault with its art for being full of hysterics and excitement, or with its newspapers for being sensational. Instead of finding fault it has every reason to be grateful—to thank a most merciful Heaven that the men in the world are still alive enough in it to be capable of feeling sensation in other men's lives, though they have ceased to be capable of having sensations in their own, or of feeling sensations if they had them.   It was when the herds of her people were buried in routine and peace that Rome had bull-fights.   New York, with its hordes of drudges, ledger-slaves, machinists, and clerks, has the New York *World*. It lasts longer than a bull-fight and it can be had every morning before a man starts off to be a machine and every evening when he gets back from being a machine—for one cent.   On Sunday a whole Colosseum fronts him and he is glutted with gore from morning until night. To a man who is a penholder by the week, or a linotype machine, or a ratchet in a factory, a fight is infinite peace.   Obedience to the command of Scripture, making the Sabbath a day of rest, is entirely relative.   Some of us are rested by taking our under-interested lives to a Sunday paper, and others are rested by taking our over-interested lives to church.   Men read dime novels in proportion as their lives are staid and mechanical.   Men whose lives are their own dime novels are bored by printed ones.   Men whose years are crowded with crises, culminations, and events, who run the most risks in business, are found with the steadiest papers in their hands.   The train-boy knows that the people who buy the biggest headlines are all on salaries and that danger and blood and thunder are being read nowadays by effeminately safe men, because it is the only way they can be had.

But it is not only the things that are left out

of men's lives but the things they have too
much of, which find their remedy in books.
They are the levers with which the morbid is
controlled. *Similia similibus curantur* may be
a dangerous principle to be applied by everybody, but thousands of men and women mulling
away on their lives and worrying themselves
with themselves, cutting a wide swath of misery
wherever they go, have suddenly stopped in a
book—have purged away jealousy and despair
and passion and nervous prostration in it. A
paper-person with melancholia is a better cure
for gloom than a live clown can be — who
merely goes about reminding people how sad
they are.

A man is often heard to say that he has
tragedy enough in his own life not to want to
go to a play for more, but this much having
been said and truly said, he almost always goes
to the play—to see how true it is. The stage
is his huge confidante. Pitying one's self is
a luxury, but it takes a great while, and one
can never do it enough. Being pitied by a
five-thousand-dollar house, and with incidental
music, all for a dollar and a half, is a sure and
quick way to cheer up. Being pitied by Victor
Hugo is a sure way also. Hardy can do people's pitying for them much better than they
can do it, and it 's soon over and done with.
It is noticeable that while the impressive books,
the books that are written to impress people,
have a fair and nominal patronage, it is the

expressive books, the books that let people out, which have the enormous sales. This seems to be true of the big-sale books whether the people expressed in them are worth expressing (to any one but themselves) or not. The principle of getting one's self expressed is so largely in evidence that not only the best but the worst of our books illustrate it. Our popular books are carbuncles mostly. They are the inevitable and irrepressible form of the instinct of health in us, struggling with disease. On the whole, it makes being an optimist in modern life a little less of a tight-rope-walk. If even the bad elements in current literature —which are discouraging enough—are making us better, what shall be said of the good?

Shelburne Essays

By Paul Elmer More

4 vols.   Crown octavo.

Sold separately.   Net, $1.25.   (By mail, $1.35)

Contents

FIRST SERIES: A Hermit's Notes on Thoreau—The Solitude of Nathaniel Hawthorne — The Origins of Hawthorne and Poe—The Influence of Emerson—The Spirit of Carlyle — The Science of English Verse — Arthur Symonds: The Two Illusions—The Epic of Ireland—Two Poets of the Irish Movement—Tolstoy; or, The Ancient Feud between Philosophy and Art—The Religious Ground of Humanitarianism.

SECOND SERIES: Elizabethan Sonnets—Shakespeare's Sonnets—Lafcadio Hearn—The First Complete Edition of Hazlitt — Charles Lamb — Kipling and FitzGerald — George Crabbe — The Novels of George Meredith — Hawthorne: Looking before and after — Delphi and Greek Literature—Nemesis; or, The Divine Envy.

THIRD SERIES: The Correspondence of William Cowper—Whittier the Poet—The Centenary of Sainte-Beuve—The Scotch Novels and Scotch History—Swinburne—Christina Rossetti—Why is Browning Popular?—A Note on Byron's "Don Juan"—Laurence Sterne—J. Henry Shorthouse—The Quest.

FOURTH SERIES: The Vicar of Morwenstow—Fanny Burney—A Note on "Daddy" Crisp—George Herbert—John Keats—Benjamin Franklin—Charles Lamb Again—Walt Whitman—William Blake—The Letters of Horace Walpole—The Theme of Paradise Lost.

A Few Press Criticisms on Shelburne Essays

" It is a pleasure to hail in **Mr.** More a genuine critic, for genuine critics in America in these days are uncommonly scarce. . . . We recommend, as a sample of his breadth, style, acumen, and power the essay on Tolstoy in the present volume. That represents criticism that has not merely a metropolitan but a world note. . . . One is thoroughly grateful to Mr. More for the high quality of his thought, his serious purpose, and his excellent style."—*Harvard Graduates' Magazine.*

"We do not know of any one now writing who gives evidence of a better critical equipment than Mr. More. It is rare nowadays to find a writer so thoroughly familiar with both ancient and modern thought. It is this width of view, this intimate acquaintance with so much of the best that has been thought and said in the world, irrespective of local prejudice, that constitute Mr. More's strength as a critic. He has been able to form for himself a sound literary canon and a sane philosophy of life which constitute to our mind his peculiar merit as a critic."—*Independent.*

"He is familiar with classical, Oriental, and English literature; he uses a temperate, lucid, weighty, and not ungraceful style; he is aware of his best predecessors, and is apparently on the way to a set of philosophic principles which should lead him to a high and perhaps influential place in criticism. . . . We believe that we are in the presence of a critic who must be counted among the first who take literature and life for their theme."—*London Speaker.*

G. P. Putnam's Sons
New York   London

CPSIA information can be obtained
at www.ICGtesting.com
Printed in the USA
BVOW06*1214081117

499867BV00011B/191/P